HE CARES

He Cares

YOU ARE NOT ALONE
WHEN NAVIGATING LOSS

MAJENDI JARRETT

FOREWORD BY
ALAN WEST

Also by Majendi Jarrett

MARLEY'S MEMOIR: THE JOURNEY TO AN IRREVERSIBLE ACTION AND THE AFTERMATH

LIVING WITHOUT MARLEY

HE CARES

MAJENDI JARRETT

Copyright © 2025 by Majendi Jarrett
All rights reserved.

Foreword copyright © 2025 by Alan West
All rights reserved.

ISBN 978-1-0685524-0-3 (paperback)
ISBN 978-1-0685524-2-7 (hardcover)
ISBN 978-1-0685524-1-0 (ebook)

No part of this book may be used or reproduced by any means, graphic, electronic or mechanical, including photocopying, recording, taping or by any information storage retrieval system without the written permission of the author except in the case of brief written quotations embodied in critical articles and reviews.

This book is a work of nonfiction. Unless otherwise noted, the author and the publisher make no explicit guarantees as to the accuracy of the information contained in this book and in some cases, names of people and places have been altered to protect their privacy.

Scripture quotations are taken from The Amplified Bible, ©1965, 2015 by The Lockman Foundation.

Cover design: Jonathan Hahn
Edited by Allison Felus

Printed worldwide through Ingram

Dedication

I would like to dedicate this book to all close family members I have lost.
And to all who have lost close family members, I would like to say that God cares—you are never alone.

Contents

Foreword		1
Acknowledgments		3
Introduction		4
1	Mum Is Coming	5
2	Gone Too Soon, or Was It?	11
3	Standing on the Word	17
4	An Offer I Could Not Resist	23
5	Embracing My New Surroundings	28
6	Settling in My New Life	33
7	Settled but Unsettled	41
8	Surprises and Challenges	48
9	First and Last Christmas	54
10	Saying Good-bye to Mum	59
11	Planning Mum's Service	65
12	Different Losses: How Do They Compare?	71
13	Marley, Always in My Heart	76
14	Final Words	82
15	Epilogue: Three Years & Nine Months Later	88

Foreword

This book approaches a subject we all would like to shy away from. No one wants to face the painful reality of grief, bereavement, and death. But the way Majendi Jarrett writes and speaks through these pages about her personal experiences of grief and bereavement are so real, and her honesty, truthfulness, and candid approach are so inspiring and humbling, that she gives hope to all of us who will one day also face the loss of someone we love.

I've personally known Majendi and her family for twenty-five years or so. I've been their pastor and friend during that time. Again, she speaks openly and candidly about her faith in God and her personal walk with Christ, which has given her the strength, faith, and courage to carry on and face tomorrow. Jesus has been her closest friend in her time of need. I've personally seen from close range how she has coped in recent years after the tragic death of her son Marley. Her faith has been a rock on which she has stood and has given hope to so many. It was Jesus Himself who taught us to build our lives on something rock solid, not on the shifting sands of this fragile world's standards, so that when the storms of life hit us, we will miraculously survive, as we are anchored to eternal truth.

I'm a father of two sons and the thought of losing one of them is too painful to contemplate. Majendi has helped me, and I know her story will help and encourage many who will face in their life's journey the reality and pain of grief and bereavement with HOPE and COURAGE.

Alan West

Retired pastor of Luton Christian Fellowship and former football player at Burnley, Luton Town, and Millwall (UK) and of the Minnesota Kicks (USA)

Acknowledgments

Above all I want to thank God for strengthening me and giving me a purpose, turning my pain to a purpose. He has given me the strength and the boldness to write this book and my other two books.

Without the support of my husband Trevor and my son Nathan, I would not have written any of the books, much more this one. Thank you, Trevor and Nathan, for your continuous love and support.

I also want to acknowledge Pastor Mike Nicholls who gave me the inspiration for the title of this book and Alan West for being so kind to write the foreword for this book.

I am grateful for the support I have received from family, friends, my church (Luton Christian Fellowship), and the BSBS (Bedfordshire Suicide Bereavement Services) during these difficult months.

I also want to thank some special people who have been constantly asking me when the third book will be released. These people do not how much they have encouraged me by just asking about it. There was a time before I started writing the third book that I thought I would only have two books in the Loss and Grief series, but then I was reminded that I had said that there will be two books after I launched my first.

Introduction

In this book I want to share about the grief and loss journeys I went through before losing my son Marley. Whilst there are similarities, there are significant differences between death by sickness and death by suicide.

I want to give insight into the circumstances and the time frame of these previous losses, how old I was both physically (since I was born) and spiritually (since I became a believer), and most importantly how God has always been there for me, even at times when it did not feel like it.

I also want to show how the closeness I shared with each person described in this book impacted me in different ways.

I want also to tell everyone who reads this book that there is hope. A transition takes place when we go through losses; we are birthed into something new. This could be a new direction, a new country, or something else.

I hope that everyone who has lost someone will be able to relate to the feelings and circumstances I share in this book.

1

Mum Is Coming

No one can escape the pain of losing someone. Sooner or later, we will all go through it. Depending on your character, losing someone you love and care for might be the hardest thing you will ever have to face, the hardest thing you will ever have to go through. When you experience it for the first time, it can be really tough. Loss can almost paralyse you, depending on how close you were to the person who passed.

My first experience of deep loss was my brother, Frank Dinsdale Bowen Wright. I lost him at the young age of twenty-nine. It was the first time I lost someone who I was not expecting to die. It was the first time I lost someone who was young. It was the first time I lost someone who was very close to me, and it was the first time that my faith as a believer was tested.

Though I had lost other family members before losing my brother, those losses did not hit me as hard. Perhaps it was because the people were not so close to me—an elderly aunt or uncle, other distant relations, or a friend's mother. However, even when I lost my dad, it was not as difficult as when I lost my brother. I think because I had never lived in the same house as my dad, I did not have the kind of really close, loving relationship with him that I did with my brother.

Frank and I grew up together. He was four years older than me, so in our teens we experienced all the same growing pains of being punished or told off by our mum because we were out late or because we did not do our chores. He was protective of me when we were out partying and young boys were trying to chat me up. We shared our teenage years together.

I have vivid memories of our home in Congo Cross, Banana Water. I remember us playing outside during the school holidays, then rushing to get indoors as soon as we spotted our mum coming home from work. I would usually be much closer to the house than Frank and my other brother Raymond because they would be doing the forbidden: playing football in the street. They were not allowed to do this, as it was not a football field and they could easily have gotten hit by a car. We used to live in the second floor of a two-storey house, so I would be downstairs, playing catchers or skipping with the neighbour's children who were closer to my age. Then suddenly I would see Frank sprinting towards me, racing up the stairs shouting, "Mum is coming!" Just thinking about it now brings a smile to my face. At 16 he was all long legs in his shorts, dashing towards the house, closely followed by Raymond. This would be my cue either to run upstairs and sit quietly with a book or to race to complete any chores that were left undone whilst we were playing with our neighbours.

If we were successful, Mum would not have a clue that we had been playing outside, and if she was in a good mood, she would even turn a blind eye to the fact that we were only just doing our chores then, when we had had the whole rest of the day to do them. We would be grinning at each other behind her back, knowing we had narrowly escaped being told off for doing exactly what she had told us not to do.

It's not that she did not want us to play outside. But there were several reasons why she discouraged us from doing so. First, she was a very quiet and introverted person and she knew that our playing outside could have led to issues with other children or neighbours, which could have created tension. Neighbours were always falling out because of their children. There was also the chance that we would mistakenly kick the football against a glass window or hit an older person with it, either of which would have meant unnecessary expenses that our mum could not afford. Also, if someone *had* gotten hit—especially an older person—they would have brought a complaint against us. As children, we did not understand these reasons. We were more concerned with our enjoyment. Fortunately, we never broke any windows or hit anyone with the ball.

On other occasions when we were not quick enough and she saw my brothers on the street playing football, we would get an earful from her. She would go on all evening until we went to bed. At the time I thought she was a party pooper, stopping us from having fun, but as I got older, I saw things a bit more from her perspective. She wanted us to be safe. Sometimes the cars were being driven too fast, and a few children had been hit by a car and ended up with a broken leg or arm, and she did not want that for us. As children we did not understand this.

I also have memories of Frank and Raymond hitting puberty and becoming very conscious of their body image. As we all grew up, we lost whatever puppy fat we had and became mostly long arms and legs. I can recall Frank and Raymond discovering that press-ups would build their muscles and competing with each other to see who could do the most. Of course, being the only girl,

I did not want to be left out of the fun, so I would also join them in doing the press-ups. Though of course I would be the first to give up because my arms were aching and I could not do anymore. Frank was very competitive and, being the eldest of the three of us, he wanted to be the one that did the most press-ups. Afterwards he would flex his muscles and show off to Raymond that he was stronger. The more press-ups they did, the more toned and more conscious of their body image they became, especially when they started attracting the attention of girls. I enjoyed a few freebies from girls who Frank dated or who wanted to be noticed by him. It was typical in those days for girls to be nice to us younger siblings so we would put in a good word for her to my brother.

I especially remember one girl who I got quite close with. She was older than me and she used to do my hair very nicely. She was very particular in the way she dressed and presented herself, and she had met Frank because they were both part of a local choir close to where we lived. I really liked her, and every time I would go to her to do my hair, I would be there a long time. So, my mum started getting very concerned. She was not happy that I had a friend who was older than me. She thought the girl would be a bad influence on me. What she did not know at the time was that I was the messenger for Frank. There were no mobile phones in those days, and we did not even have a landline at home. So, when I went by her to do my hair, I would pass messages to her from Frank, and she would give me a message for him in return. Usually, he was letting her know that he would be at choir practice so they could see each other.

Unfortunately, their relationship did not last very long because she became very jealous and possessive over Frank. He attracted a lot of girls because of his musical talent. (His dad had been a talented musician, so I believe he inherited his talents from him.)

Even though he was not interested in these other girls, she was not happy with his having any of these friendships with them, so they split up. She and I continued to be friends until Mum put a stop to it and told me that I had to get someone else closer to my age to do my hair.

As I said, Frank was a very talented musician. He could play the organ, piano, clarinet, and trombone, to name a few of the many instruments he had played. He was part of a few choirs and bands because of his talent. I used to enjoy watching and listening to him play the clarinet at home, as this was one of the instruments he could take with him after practice, whilst I could only see and hear him play the organ when we went to church as we did not have a piano at home. He had very long and slender fingers and they would race across the keyboard as if it was magic, and you would hear all these beautiful notes. I always thought that he was going to be famous and travel the world because of his musical talent.

Whilst we had a lot of good times, it would not be a normal childhood if we did not have our sibling squabbles. Like any normal family, we had our ups and downs. We did fall out a few times. Usually, it was over food, as food was always scarce when we were young. As teenagers, my brothers had big appetites. We were always fighting over food. Either one person's portion was too big or they had eaten someone else's share. Also, Frank, being the eldest son of the three of us, was very big on respect, and he would not tolerate Raymond or I being disrespectful to him. Kissing our teeth at him—a very common way to disrespect someone in the African community—would get him very angry. Also, when food was scarce, if we ate anything of his, this would not go down well. It would be a time of testing out the muscles Frank and Raymond had developed from the press-ups. Sometimes I would try to intervene between the two of them and would be at the receiving end of some punches in the crossfire. It definitely made me wiser, though, and gave me a better understanding of how to throw punches.

I will never forget one Christmas Eve when Frank and Raymond had decided to go out clubbing. Mum had told them they had to be back before midnight. Since they did not have keys to the house, they had to be back before she locked the door for the night. At that time, I was still too young to be allowed to go out with them; they must have been seventeen and nineteen and I was only fifteen. They stayed out beyond their curfew and Mum locked the door so that they could not get in. They threw some rocks at the window to get my attention so I could open the door and let them in, but Mum had hidden the key. They stayed outside until about 2 am before she finally let them in. Then they had to endure a telling-off that would go on for hours. It did not matter that it was so early in the morning. Later we had to go to our aunt's home for Christmas dinner, so the telling-off would go up another level, as they would now be told off by our aunts and our grandmother and any other older relative who had been invited to the holiday meal.

I always felt protected by my brothers, though, especially by Raymond as we went to the same primary school. He used to fight anyone who wanted to take advantage of me. When I was old enough to go out at night, I always had either Frank or Raymond with me. I was never on my own, and I loved it. It was great to have two brothers close to my age, though it also had its disadvantages, as most of the boys who were attracted to me were not brave enough to approach me because of my brothers. But I did not mind, because I thought if a boy really cared, he would be man enough to not be put off by my brothers.

2

Gone Too Soon, or Was It?

I became a believer in and follower of our Lord Jesus Christ when I was in my second year at university in Sierra Leone. I had heard messages about salvation a number of times, but a series of events that happened around this time caused everything to finally click.

I had always been concerned about being one of those believers who accepted Jesus as their personal saviour but then did not show any fruits or character worthy of the Lord. This was one of the reasons why it took me so long; I used to look at other believers and the way they acted and I would be the judge and jury, condemning them for not living the life of a believer. Even though I was not a believer, I would judge them on what I thought a believer should or should not do. This was something that God had to deal with me on personally to ensure that I took the step of faith. It was my own personal relationship with God and nobody else's that Jesus was concerned about. I cannot say it was because of this person or that person that I had not received my salvation for which Jesus had paid the price. It was also not guaranteed that, by putting it off, I would be ready, that I would not run out of time. As tomorrow is not promised to us, we have today and we have now. We need to open our hearts and not keep saying *I will do it tomorrow* or *next week* or *next year, after I have done this, that, or the other*. The Bible says,

"Do not harden your hearts as [your fathers did] in the rebellion [of Israel at Meribah], On the day of testing in the wilderness" (Hebrews 3:8).

I was definitely hardening my heart against taking the step of faith prior to my second year at university. Once I received the revelation that I was trying to do things in my own strength and not leaning on God, I felt better. I realised that I can only do this through Christ who strengthens me, as it says in these verses:

"I can do all things [which He has called me to do] through Him who strengthens *and* empowers me [to fulfill His purpose—I am self-sufficient in Christ's sufficiency; I am ready for anything and equal to anything through Him who infuses me with inner strength and confident peace]" (Philippians 4:13).

Once I said the sinner's prayer, I was committed. I hungered and thirsted for the things of God. I attended a Saturday Bible school that was next door to where I lived. I learnt a lot and fed my spirit with the word of God, which enabled my faith to grow very strong.

I looked forward to the weekends: I would get home from university on Friday then I would spend Saturday at Bible school and Sunday in church. I was committed. I could not get enough of the word of God, the preaching, the praise and worship. I also started attending an all-night prayer meeting on Friday nights with a few friends, and I was seeing the word of God coming to life at those events. Being a new believer, I did not think there was anything I could ask God for, according to His word, that I would not receive. Don't get me wrong—I still believe that now, but I have more context than I did then. I know that God's will and purpose for me also plays a very important part in what I receive when I ask. I was raw and new and on fire, and I wanted everyone who could listen to hear what Jesus did for us and how He changed my life.

Before my final year at university, I experienced a big change in my life. My mum moved to England because my stepdad was sick and dying of cancer. Since Frank had moved out when he got married and my other brother Raymond was living with our aunt, before my mum left for England, she made plans for me to live with some of our other relations whom I had grown close to in recent years.

Frank would always arrange transportation for me when I needed to go back to campus after summer vacation and this time was no different. I had reached out to him the weekend before my birthday both to arrange my transportation and to invite him to my birthday celebrations; I was planning to have a few close friends and family round for my birthday and I was expecting that he, his wife, and their nine-month-old daughter would attend.

On that Saturday he arrived as planned with a jeep that belonged to one of his numerous friends. The driver helped load the vehicle with my luggage and we were off. I noticed that he looked a bit pale and I asked if he was all right. He more or less brushed the question off. So, we talked about my birthday, which was coming up that Wednesday, and he said he would try to make the party after work with his wife and daughter. When we arrived at my campus, he helped me unload and put my stuff in my dormitory. I hugged him and thanked him for his help and told him I would see him that Wednesday for my birthday. I did not know that was the last time I would see him alive.

On Tuesday, the day before my birthday, I heard from Frank's wife that he was not feeling well and would not be able to attend the birthday celebrations I had planned for Wednesday. He was going to see the doctor because his feet were swollen, and they would do some tests. At the time I did not think too much of it. It was normal for people to be unwell and go see the doctor, then everything would be fine. I had no idea the seriousness of what my brother was facing combined with the challenges of having a very poor health care system in Sierra Leone.

The next day I still had a few friends round for my birthday, but in the midst of it I received a call informing me that things were really serious with Frank. He needed dialysis, which was not available at that time in Sierra Leone. His kidney had failed and he was in hospital. I could not believe what I was hearing. For some reason it felt as if I were hearing news about somebody else, not the brother who I had just seen, spoken to, and hugged, who had promised to be at my birthday party. *It cannot be. How could things have deteriorated so quickly since the last time I saw him, not even a week before?* These were just some of the thoughts running through my mind.

The birthday celebration was cut short, and we made our way to the hospital. But unfortunately, I could not see him because he had been sedated. The doctors, his wife, and our family discussed the best way forward. I thought about mum who had travelled to England less than a year ago and wondered how she must be feeling. She had been contacted by her sister, my aunt, who was a doctor and understood all the medical challenges Frank was facing.

There was talk at that time of flying him to Ghana, as they had more advanced health care than Sierra Leone. There was also talk of getting a dialysis machine from England, but it needed to be done immediately. Time was of the essence. All these various plans of action were being discussed but none of them could happen immediately, and I thought *I need to pray*. I needed God to come through for us in this time of need. I was still a new believer and I took God at His word. I felt that I had to stand in the gap and pray through the night for Frank to get better, as only God could bring him through this. We were hitting a lot of roadblocks to get him the care that he needed, but God who is the healer would put everything right.

I can remember that Thursday night so vividly. I was staying in my cousin's spare room, as I could not be at university with all this going on. I started praying, speaking to God my Father about Frank and what I wanted Him to do. I was interceding for a miracle, praying that above all odds Frank would be healed, that this was not the end. I thought about his nine-month-old daughter and his wife; I thought about my mum and our family; I thought about all the talent Frank had and how God could use him further. I had also heard that the pastor who hosted the all-night prayer service my cousin and I had been attending had befriended Frank and his wife and had visited him in hospital. And I prayed, crying to the Lord to heal him. I interceded into the early hours of the morning because I did not feel the peace I craved. I did not yet feel that all would be well, that we would not lose Frank at the young age of twenty-nine, so soon after he had gotten married and had a child. I thought he would pull through. When I had no more tears and my voice was hoarse, I stopped praying and went to bed.

The next morning was a Friday, and I went back to the hospital. I had heard from my aunt that the medical team was going to try something different to help him, so I was hopeful. I really believed that this was the answer to my prayers. I remember pacing outside the ward, praying and trusting God for a miracle.

I will never forget seeing my aunt coming toward us to tell us that Frank was gone. So many emotions went through me. At first I could not say anything. Then I got really angry. I could not believe that God would take him when he had a nine-month-old daughter who needed him. I also felt let down. I had prayed through the night for healing and God had not answered my prayers.

What do you do when you pray and stand on God's word yet it feels as if God has not answered your prayer? The simple answer is that you continue to trust God that He knows best. Though it is hard, and in your heart you feel angry or disappointed, you have to trust God. He knows what is best. We do not have the answers from the master plan. To me, and to most people, it seemed that Frank's life was cut short. But he probably achieved more in twenty-nine years than most people do if they live to be one hundred. We are all here to achieve the purpose God has for us. For some of us, this takes fewer years than it takes for others.

At Frank's funeral it became very clear that he had touched a lot of lives through the numerous organisations he had been part of. He had played clarinet and other instruments as a member of his secondary school's band, and later he had been the organist at a lot of weddings, funerals, choir festivals, and thanksgiving services. He had made himself available to so many churches, choirs, musical groups, and associations. He had also started teaching music to the next generation. It was part of his side hustle, but what he may not have realized at the time is that he was passing on his legacy to future musicians. He was revered at his funeral. There were people of all ages paying homage to how he had positively affected their lives.

3

Standing on the Word

As a young believer when you have that newborn faith, it can be very hard to understand why God answers some prayers but other prayers don't seem to be answered the way we wanted or requested. I was zealous for the things of God. I believed the verses in the Bible when Jesus said

"Until now you have not asked [the Father] for anything in My name; but now ask *and* keep on asking and you will receive, so that your joy may be full *and* complete" (John 16:24).

I believed that when I prayed and asked God to heal Frank in Jesus's name that it should be done. What I did not grasp or understand was God's will in that situation. I did not understand about God's ways and our ways. As Isaiah 55:8–9 says,

"'For My thoughts are not your thoughts, Nor are your ways My ways,' declares the Lord. 'For as the heavens are higher than the earth, So are My ways higher than your ways And My thoughts *higher* than your thoughts.'"

When you put your trust in God and you are knocked back because, in your eyes, your prayer was not answered, it is very hard to move forward if you don't have some understanding of why. I had to understand that, whilst I prayed for Frank to be healed, I did not have the bigger picture; only God had that bigger picture. It took time for me to start to understand that God had a plan for Frank's wife and his daughter that would take them away from Sierra Leone, that this event would trigger plans for them to move to England.

It is understandable that, after Frank's loss, I would be really shaken and would have doubts that God is who He says He is. *How could God let my nine-month-old niece be fatherless and my sister-in-law a widow?* These were some of the questions that I did not have answers to. I did not understand how a loving God could take away someone who was so young and had so much to live for. I was going through the motions of reading my Bible and going to church, but I was angry with God. But that was the plan of the enemy.

I was glad I did not stop going to church or reading my Bible, because it was through this that God was able to take away the anger and disappointment that I had. He reminded me about what had previously stopped me from becoming a committed believer: looking at other people who professed to be believers and seeing that they were not living according to God's word. He reminded me that I had said I would look to Him, and not to others, and this included looking at Frank. I had been setting my heart and my whole perspective around Frank, and that was taking my eyes away from God. As it says in the Bible:

"Let us run with endurance *and* active persistence the race that is set before us, [looking away from all that will distract us and] focusing our eyes on Jesus, who is the Author and Perfecter of faith [the first incentive for our belief and the One who brings our faith to maturity], who for the joy [of accomplishing the goal] set before Him endured the cross, disregarding the shame, and sat down at the right hand of the throne of God [revealing His deity, His authority, and the completion of His work] (Hebrews 12:1–2).

I was fixing my eyes on Frank and not on Jesus. Every time I focused on Frank and his passing and how young he was, I became angry and disappointed. But when I fixed my eyes on Jesus, I remembered that Jesus died for me. He lived on this earth as a man for thirty-three years, and again, in our human thinking, we would say He left too soon, there was more that He could have accomplished. But Jesus had done what He had to do and therefore He had to go. If God could not spare His own son Jesus who was sinless, how could I expect Him to let Frank be here beyond the purpose that God had for him? Frank had accomplished what he was here for, and therefore he passed. He had served his purpose.

The more I fixed my eyes on Jesus, the stronger I got and the more bearable my loss became. I know that God loves each and every one of us, and He loves us more than we love ourselves, more than we love each other. If He did not love us, He would not have sent Jesus, His only son, to die for us. Did I love Frank more than God loved him? Definitely not. Did I want the best plans for Frank more than God? Definitely not. In the Bible it says,

"For You formed my innermost parts; You knit me [together] in my mother's womb" (Psalm 139:13).

What does this mean? It means that God knows us. He gave us our DNA. He made us to be who we are and put a plan together for when we would be born and when we will die. He knows us inside out. His plan for us is good:

"For we are His workmanship [His own master work, a work of art], created in Christ Jesus [reborn from above—spiritually transformed, renewed, ready to be used] for good works, which God prepared [for us] beforehand [taking paths which He set], so that we would walk in them [living the good life which He prearranged and made ready for us]" (Ephesians 2:10).

God wants us to accomplish that plan because He loves us. He cares. I might not always like the direction that God leads me because I don't see the ending when He starts leading me. But I need to trust His leading, because He cares for me and because His plan for me is always good. He will always lead me in the right path toward what is best for me.

All of us have an earthly father who would, in most cases, care for us and want the best for us, though sometimes we would disagree with him because we want to do things our own way. Yet sometimes, because of his experience, he would know that the decisions we are making are the wrong ones and would try to steer us in the right direction by withholding things from us. A father does not do this because he does not care, but because he can see what lies ahead.

I thought Frank could have accomplished so many wonderful things as a musician. I had an image of him becoming an international musician, touring the world, entertaining audiences in different locations playing Handel's *Messiah*. I had so many wishes for him and now he was gone.

I would like all my friends and family to live long and fulfilling lives, but who determines the length of our time here on earth? Definitely not us. God determines how long we will be here, and it is important that we are living according to His will and His plan for our lives. It starts with believing in the Lord Jesus Christ and what He did at Calvary. Jesus died for our sins, and He died in our place so that if we believed in Him we would not perish but have everlasting life. If you belong to another faith, pray that God speaks to your heart. Let him lead you. If you don't believe that there is a God, then think again, meditate on these words, and listen to what your heart is saying to you.

We are all here on earth to fulfil God's purpose for us. Some of us have a longer time to do this, while others have a shorter time. It is important that, whilst we are here, we live for God, because after this life, there is eternity. I know that there are many beliefs regarding this, but I am holding on to what the Bible says:

"For God so [greatly] loved *and* dearly prized the world that He [even] gave His [One and] only begotten Son, so that whoever believes *and* trusts in Him [as Savior] shall not perish, but have eternal life. For God did not send the Son into the world to judge *and* condemn the world [that is, to initiate the final judgment of the world], but that the world might be saved through Him" (John 3:16–17).

I cannot tell you about God's love and how He cares for me without sharing the ultimate sacrifice that God made in letting his one and only Son, Jesus, die for you and me. We are all sinners, and the only sacrifice that could atone for our sins was the death of Jesus. When Jesus died, He paid the price for you and for me. He paid the price for Frank and for everyone who was yet to be born.

My comfort is that I will be reunited in heaven with Frank and all loved ones who died as believers. This is not the end. As it says in the Bible:

"Jesus said to her, 'I am the Resurrection and the Life. Whoever believes in (adheres to, trusts in, relies on) Me [as Savior] will live even if he dies'" (John 11:25).

There is a life better than this. Jesus promises us that, if we believe in Him, though we die in the flesh, we will continue to live, because our spirit leaves this earthly body. We are then reunited with our Heavenly Father. This life is not the end for all of us who believe in Jesus. So, if you are reading this and you have not taken that step of faith yet, this is your opportunity to do so.

4

An Offer I Could Not Resist

Frank's passing triggered a change in my future plans. The following year my aunt decided that it would be good for me to visit my mum in England, as she was grieving for Frank all by herself, without any of her other children with her. She had not come over for Frank's funeral since it is not the custom of Sierra Leoneans for parents to attend the funerals of their children. I think it is the custom for most West African countries that the parents, especially the mothers, do not attend the burials of their children. It had cost a lot of money for her to go to England and she was still in the process of sorting out her late husband's estate. So, it made sense for one of us to go over and spend some time with her.

When my aunt told me that she planned to take me with her during the summer months to visit my mum, my first thought was that I would stay with my mum. I would live with her in England and not come back to Sierra Leone. I had just finished university in Freetown and had earned my degree in Linguistics and Religious

Studies. I had not yet applied for any jobs, so it was the ideal time for me to start a new life in another country. There was no promise of a job to keep me in Freetown, so I started seeing this as an opportunity that would open doors for me. I was excited to be going over to see my mum; we were very close and it had been over a year since she had left for England. I remember speaking to her when she learnt that my aunt was bringing me over to see her. She was so excited. She had been so sad after the loss of my brother, so it was a good thing that my aunt came up with this perfect plan.

Before my mum went to England, I was one of few people I knew who had had no desire to live in another country. I had no desire to live in Europe or in America. I had aspirations to travel but not to live abroad. At that time, I loved living in Sierra Leone even though things were not great there and even though I always heard about the opportunities for education and career progress that could be attained in the Western part of the world. Yet during my early teenage years, the idea of leaving did not appeal to me. Perhaps it was because of the high crime rates elsewhere. I constantly heard news of murders and attacks from friends and family who had already left, and it seemed very scary to me.

Apart from the occasional protests against the government, there was nothing scary that happened in Sierra Leone. (Of course, this was way before the tragedy of the guerilla warfare that started in 1997 in Freetown.) Although on one occasion when I used to live with my cousin and his wife and family, there was a coup. He was in the army so we used to live in the army quarters. I remember that we had to be smuggled from the quarters late at night to stay with another relative who lived far away from there. Since at the time my cousin did not know if it would be a peaceful coup, it was important to take precautions and move our family away from the quarters for safety. If it was not peaceful, we would have been in danger. At the time it was a very scary situation, but when we were later told that the coup had been peaceful and all was calm, we moved back to the army quarters. That was my only scary moment when I was in Sierra Leone. I was glad that I was not there when the guerilla war started, as I have heard of so many scary encounters with the rebels and the atrocities that people went through. I do not know how I would have survived that, but God in His mercy brought me over to England so I did not have to go through it.

I also had this wrong idea that believers in very developed countries were not as committed as those of us who were in underdeveloped and developing countries. I believed that our faith was stronger because we did not have access to most things and therefore did not take anything for granted. Whether it was health care, social care, or the higher cost of living, we had to trust God for everything. I have since learnt that there are believers with strong faith and commitment in the western part of the world, just as there were in Sierra Leone before I left. I believe I was still being delivered from the judgemental spirit that had been stopping me from making a commitment to Jesus. There was a part of me that thought I would fall into the trap of depending on material things rather than on Jesus, as had so many of the believers I knew once they left Sierra Leone. I was also concerned that I would not be able to find a Bible-believing church like the one I had been attending and that this would likewise lead to my fall away from grace. When I think of it now, I realised how naïve and uneducated about the churches and believers in the western part of the world I was.

These were the thoughts I had held onto before the grief and the loss and then the opportunity to be reunited with my mum came knocking at my door. There is something you should know about me and my mum: we had a very close relationship. My mum told me that well before she ever got pregnant, she wanted a daughter. Part of the reason was because when she was a teenager, she had been a babysitter for some of the neighbour's children and they were all girls and she had loved taking care of them. When she got married and got pregnant with her first child, she hoped she would have a girl. Six pregnancies later she finally had me, her only daughter. Don't get me wrong; she loved every boy child she had and never showed any favouritism to me over my brothers. But I definitely knew I was loved. At the same time, she did not let me get away with anything. She was a very strict disciplinarian, and I believe that some of that definitely rubbed off me. The thought of living with her again really took away all the negative thoughts I had previously had about being a believer in the western world.

Before she had come over to England, life had been tough for us. There were days when we did not know where our next meal would come from. There were times when Mum had to sell her own clothes to be able to put food on the table for us. She had retired at the age of fifty-five, which, at that time, was the standard age for retirement for government employees in Sierra Leone. She had planned on living on a combination of her retirement payout and income from a hat-making business she had started. Unfortunately, she had had to use most, if not all, of her retirement money on an unexpected situation, which left her without those funds. The demand for hats also dried up, which meant that sales from her custom shop also became unreliable. The two of us had even been given eviction notice because the landlady whose house we were renting wanted it for other uses. When Mum went to England, it was a godsend. Indeed, the Bible says,

"And we know [with great confidence] that God [who is deeply concerned about us] causes all things to work together [as a plan]

for good for those who love God, to those who are called according to His plan *and* purpose" (Romans 8:28).

God had a plan for us, and that plan was leading to a life away from Sierra Leone. It turned out I would have many more opportunities in England than I would have had in Sierra Leone. I was excited about the future, even though there was so much to do before my departure. For example, I did not have a passport, as I had never gone outside of Sierra Leone before, and there were vaccines to take care of as well. It was painful to say good-bye to my brothers, my close friends, and my grandmother, as I did not know when I would see them again. But this sadness was mixed with the anticipation of flying on an aeroplane for the first time and the joy of reuniting with my mum again. It was a bittersweet but very exciting time for me.

5

Embracing My New Surroundings

I left Freetown, Sierra Leone, on 5 August 1993. After about an hour layover in Amsterdam, I arrived at Heathrow Airport in London on the morning of 6 August 1993, then took a shuttle to Gatwick. I would be staying with another aunt in Surrey for the weekend before making my way to Bedfordshire on the following Monday. I remember speaking to Mum on the phone and feeling so happy because I would be seeing her in a couple of days. It felt surreal to finally be there.

Meanwhile, that Saturday, I had a wedding to attend, along with my cousin who had accompanied me on this trip. We were planning to take the train there and back. My aunt who lived in Surrey was very knowledgeable about what trains we should take and where we should connect, so it was like we had our own personal information board. Unfortunately, in those days there were no mobile phones, so if we got stuck, we would have to find a phone box to make a call. Unlike nowadays, there were still plenty of those around, so it would not be a problem, as long as we had the necessary coins to make the call. How times have changed compared to then; now everyone has a mobile phone with easy access to all train stations, train times, and connections.

My cousin and I dressed in our traditional outfits for the wedding and received repeated instructions from both aunties on what to do and who to talk to if we needed information. I could understand my aunts' concern, as they had promised my mum that we would be with her that coming Monday. And of course, the last thing my aunt wanted was to have to tell Mum that something had happened to me, especially after the loss of my brother. If it had been up to my mum, she would have preferred for us to go directly to Bedfordshire, as she could not wait to see me. But after about the hundredth reminder of what to do and what not do enroute, since this was our first time in this strange country, we set off.

It's funny how we use the term "strange" so loosely when we are not familiar with something. Anything that is different or unfamiliar we tend to label as strange. This was an especially common use of the word for those of us from Sierra Leone, particularly in those days.

My auntie had attained her medical qualifications in England and Scotland and went on to become the first female gynaecologist in Freetown, Sierra Leone. She was a member of a few international organisations and was a seasoned traveller. But it was exciting stepping out in England for the first time without her. My cousin and I were two adults; how hard could it be if we followed the clear instructions we had been given? It should be easy peasy. We did make a few wrong turns, and we received some stares from passersby who were not used to seeing people in full African attire, but we eventually found our way to the wedding and enjoyed ourselves. The bride and groom were Sierra Leoneans, so there were a lot of Sierra Leoneans there. At least we fit in quite well there in our traditional African attire.

On the way back, we had to wait for a while for our train. Since there were two of us, we did not feel too intimidated being on the platform with only a handful of others. Still, because it took a while before the train came, we wondered if it would have been better if we had left a bit earlier, but we had been enjoying ourselves at the wedding. When we got off the train at the end of the journey, we had a bit of a walk before getting back to our aunt's house. But again, because we had each other, it was not so frightening. Our aunts were relieved when we arrived home safely.

I was inwardly satisfied that we had navigated the whole journey on the train without someone else accompanying us. When we came to England, trains and escalators were new phenomena, as we did not have either of them in Sierra Leone. Getting money out of a hole in the wall from a cash machine was likewise unfamiliar. We tried not to look around with wonder and amazement at all the spectacular things that residents of England take for granted.

On Sunday, we went to London for sightseeing. My aunt was familiar with the journey, as it was one she had made several times. My cousin and I could relax and left all the navigation to her. It was great to visit all the famous places that we had heard so much about: Big Ben, Oxford Circus, Harrods, and Buckingham Palace, to name just a few. We did not have time to explore each sight; this was just a chance to see the familiar places that we had heard so much about. I felt at the time that our aunt wanted to see these places through our eyes—not that she was jaded, but because she had been to London so often, it had become overly familiar to her. Whilst for us, this was all very new.

When we boarded the big red double-decker buses, we experienced firsthand the politeness of our fellow passengers. That really made it feel like we were in another world, which, to a certain extent, we were. It was very unusual not to experience a lot of pushing and shoving, as it was the norm in Sierra Leone for everyone to fight their way onto the bus. But in London, people were very well mannered, forming orderly queues to get on the bus. When we needed to get off the bus, we did not have to scream at the top of our voices to let the driver know that we wanted him or her to stop at the next bus stop. All we had to do was press the bell, which would alert the driver that there were passengers who needed to get off at the next stop.

It was also a warm day with lots of people out sightseeing, so we fit in quite well with the other tourists looking with wonder at Big Ben. We had heard so much about this famous sight, and now we got to be there in person, looking at it in awe. I also looked at the pedestrian crossings and zebra crossings with amazement, though I now take them for granted. There were no pedestrian crossings or zebra crossing where I had come from, so this was all a novelty to me.

Even in those first few days, my image and perspective of England started to change. I realised that I had dwelled too much on its negative aspects without considering the positive aspects of what I had heard or been told. As I said earlier, I had had an image of a place full of criminals killing innocent people. I could see then that it was different. One could walk around and do normal things without being killed. There were people who smiled at you and said pleasantries about the weather. I also noticed that people were very willing to help if you needed directions. I also learnt that you needed to receive the directions cautiously, as a five-minute walk for one person could be a thirty-minute walk for me.

Whilst my perspective and idea of England was changing, I still missed the family and friends I had left in Sierra Leone. Yet already

I felt that I could make this work. I could make a life here, if that was what God wanted for me.

6

Settling in My New Life

On Monday 9 August, my aunt, my cousin, and I travelled by train to Bedfordshire to meet my mum. I was so excited to see her, and she was just as excited to meet with us. It felt as if it had been years since I last saw her, even though it was less than two years. When we got off the train, we took a taxi to the house my mum lived in. I remember how wonderful it was to be hugged by mum. She had put on weight; she looked healthy and so much younger. Life in England had definitely been good for her. Although she had lost Frank, she did not seem worse off in appearance. I knew it was all internal. I was very happy to see her looking so well.

I remember that when we were growing up in Sierra Leone, she would tell us about England. She told us about the politeness and discipline of the people and about all the places she visited whilst she was living there and studying. She had always longed for the life she had left in England. She had craved the anonymity of living there with everyone minding their own business.

During that first week while my aunt and cousin from Sierra Leone stayed in Bedfordshire with us, I also reunited with another very close cousin of mine. I always marvel at how amazing God is, how He brings key people into your life at certain points in time. This cousin, Sophia, had been introduced to us by Frank when we were in Sierra Leone. Frank had first met her while he was out with some friends, and because of the uniqueness of her last name, which was also our mum's last name, he immediately knew that there was a family connection there. He invited her to visit our mum, and this led to a reunion with key members of our family. She became a very important person in all our lives, but especially mine. She even lived with us for a time when we were all in Sierra Leone, and for me it was like having a sister. We could share all sorts of girly stuff about boys that I could not share with my brothers or my mum. We developed a very strong bond that even my mum became a little jealous of. We would go everywhere and do everything together, and we were always whispering and giggling together as teenage girls do. Of course, because we were giggling about stuff mum should not hear, we would immediately go quiet when she was near, and not surprisingly, she was not happy about it. It was really bittersweet for me when Sophia had to return to her home and later on moved to England. I had missed her terribly. To be in the same place with her once again was a godsend. She was the person responsible for Mum moving to Bedfordshire and now also for me making this place my new home.

My aunt and cousin stayed with us for a week before they returned to London, though they would visit us again before going back to Sierra Leone. Mum and I settled into a routine. We were living in a shared house and she was still sorting out financial stuff after the death of her husband. It did not matter where we were, though, as long as we had each other. And I also had my cousin Sophia, who was now married with a son. I could spend time with her when I needed I change of scenery.

Mum was so happy to introduce me to the members of her church. Whilst she had been in England, she had become a believer and her faith had grown. She had told everyone in church about me and my faith, and I definitely felt that she could not wait to show me off to everyone. I didn't mind as long as it helped her in the grieving process for my brother. She had told me of all the support that she received from the pastor and his wife and the other members of the church. She did not want for anything. There was always someone there to support her.

On Sunday mornings there was someone who would collect us for church, then someone else would take us home. Usually there was also an evening service so someone would collect us for that and would also take us home again. There was a midweek prayer meeting in one of the church members' homes, so there would be someone to give us a lift to that house. There would be someone who would take me to Bible study and take me home afterwards. It was like meeting extended family members that I never knew I had. It definitely gave me a different perspective on what I had thought about the churches and believers in England. The church was Bible believing with committed members. It was not just about the preaching and teaching; their actions showed they were living it. Don't get me wrong; I missed my church in Sierra Leone. I missed the way of life in Freetown, the friends I had left behind, and the members of my family, especially my brother Raymond because we were very close. I remember writing long letters to him about what life was like in England and how I missed my life in Sierra Leone.

A few friends of mine had also moved to England, and I reconnected with them. They lived in London, so I would often go to the city for weekends to have a change of scenery and to be with friends who I had shared a lot with. I was also thinking of my next steps, as I was totally dependent on Mum. She was the sole breadwinner, though I had earned some money-making bridesmaid dresses for one of the ladies who got married soon after I arrived from Sierra Leone. Mum had been blowing my trumpet about how good a dressmaker I was although I had only made two bridesmaid dresses previously in Sierra Leone before I got pulled in to making four bridesmaid dresses of different sizes for people who I barely knew. The pressure was definitely on, as I needed to do something to earn money.

There were a few ladies in church who needed a minder for their young children whilst they were at work. They first approached Mum, who then told me about this opportunity to earn some pocket money. Since I was still unfamiliar with the town, they offered to collect me so I would not have to find my way there and back. And, as they were friends, they would get all the children (seven of them, ranging in age from two to twelve) into one home After a conversation with both families, I agreed and started child-minding for them two to three days a week. It was a no-brainer.

It was exhausting, especially chasing after the little ones to make sure that they were safe and keeping them away from danger. In those days there were not so many regulations around child-minding at home, so it was easier, though sometimes I had difficulty understanding what the children were saying. I was still trying to get my head around their regional English accent that didn't pronounce the letter *t*.

On some days I helped prepare dinner. Some of the dishes, like leg or shoulder of lamb or beef, were new and unfamiliar to me. My friend would prepare the meat then tell me when to put it in the oven and for how long. Or she would season the meat the night before, so all I had to do was put it in the oven. Then it would be ready when she got home.

Over time my confidence in the kitchen grew, but then I had a setback. My friend had started preparing a traditional Caribbean soup. The meat was still tough and needed more cooking so it could get soft. That was not a problem. If all I had to do was cook it until it was soft, I could do that. But she also wanted me to make dumplings the Jamaican way. First of all, I had never even heard of dumplings that go in soup, so I definitely did not know how to make them. She told me it was easy: flour and water were the key ingredients, to which I would add some sugar, then mould them into a round or oval shape and put them in the pot of soup. I thought, *How hard can this be?* I did not foresee any problems. I thought I had followed the instructions carefully, but the end result was not the same and of course it was difficult to convince the children that these were the dumplings they knew and loved. They looked nothing like their mum's dumplings. They did not have the right shape. From then on I never made dumplings again. Even now, years later, I ask my husband to make dumplings. There are a few other stories like the dumpling episode, and they were good lessons in life skills in my new environment.

In those early days when I could not work officially, as I was on a holiday visa, the money I got from childminding was handy. It enabled me to have some independence and not be totally dependent on Mum for everything. It also increased my knowledge of all the daytime soaps and children's programmes. I became well versed in who was who on *Neighbours* and *Home and Away*, two of the Australian soaps that the children loved watching after school. I also got acquainted with *Byker Grove*, a children's TV series that aired between 1989 and 2006, featuring the duo Ant and Dec who at the time played the characters PJ and Duncan in the series.

Looking back at my brief time as a child minder, I learnt a lot from the two families that helped me when I later became a mum.

Their values and the way they did stuff were important life lessons. They had strict routines for the younger ones that I had to adhere to. One of these was making sure that they had afternoon naps, as this prevented them from becoming very irritable around dinnertime. It was foreign to me to put a child to bed when they were not sleepy. But I trusted their judgement as parents and followed their routine, and I was pleasantly surprised that the young ones did go to sleep. There were three of them under the age of five; the other four were in school so I only watched them after school when they got dropped off by one of the parents who had a flexible shift as a dental nurse.

I will always be grateful to both families for trusting me with their precious children in those early days. I was practically a stranger when I first started, with no formal education on childminding. They knew my mum, and the same trust they had in her they likewise bestowed on me, her daughter. They also bought me my first winter coat. I had arrived in England during the summer, but it was autumn when I started childminding, with winter fast approaching. In those days it was bitterly cold with freezing temperatures and a lot of snow. I had been wearing one of Mum's winter coats, which was functional, but not many young women in their twenties would have been caught dead in it. I did not care—or I thought I did not, until I received my brand-new coat. Then I saw the difference.

After five months of childminding, I applied for and was granted a two-year working visa. In those days the UK government would give working visas to citizens of a commonwealth country. I hoped to get an office job with the degree I had from home, but nothing was forthcoming. I registered with an agency and did temporary work for another three months, which helped me get very familiar with the roads and streets, as I was always the last one to be dropped off by the agency's minibus. I was fascinated by the different names of the routes, trying to understand the difference between an avenue, a drive, and a way, since these terms were unfamiliar to me. After three months of working in different places, I finally secured a permanent staff position as a packer at a tablet manufacturing and packaging company.

One of the things that stood out for me after working in so many different environments was how normal it was for people to swear. I was not used to this. I don't remember the people around me using profanities willy-nilly in normal conversation when I was in Sierra Leone. I had never sworn, and I didn't understand why sometimes every other word in someone's conversation was a swear word. I struggled with it. It really disturbed my spirit being around people who swore all the time. After a few months of working there, I had to say something. The colleagues I worked with had noticed that I don't swear, and they wanted to know why. This was my first opportunity to share my faith with them.

Most of them were older than me and had worked there for years, some of them for more than twenty years. As time passed, they accepted that I was different, that I was a believer, so most of the older ones would refrain from swearing if I was around or near them. I would share about church and God when the opportunity arose. I also realised that a very common topic of discussion, apart from the weather, was about what would you be doing at the weekend. As soon as it was coming to the end of the working week, that would be the question that would be asked by anyone whom I was working with. Of course, my weekend always involved church, so I would use that opportunity to plant seeds of faith. Some would listen and ask more questions; some had concluded that it was "one of those happy-clappy churches" and would avoid asking me anymore questions about church. My purpose was not to "save" anyone, as only God could do that. My purpose was to plant seeds and to lead a life that was a testimony of a believer in Christ. I believed that God would do the rest.

One of the things I was quickly learning at that time was that most people who I came across in the working environment did not go to church, did not have anything to do with church, and moreover did not even believe that there is God. This was a shock to me, as everyone that had crossed my path in Sierra Leone believed in God. They may have been a Christian, a Muslim, or a Jehovah's Witness, and even if they were not one of those, they still believed there was a God. Being around people who did not believe at all was new for me. I realised in those early days that only God can give someone the revelation of who He is. I could only sow seeds of faith and share my testimony of how I came to be a believer.

I felt that I left a good impression of a believer. In fact, after I left that job to go back to college for additional education, I would meet a few of them in later years, and they were very happy to see me and would ask me about church. I continue to remember them in prayer, asking that God would reveal Himself to them and that the seeds of faith I planted in them would be watered by someone else.

7

Settled but Unsettled

Four years later, I had definitely settled into the British way of life. I could understand the regional accent where I lived much better though I still struggled with other regional accents (for example, the Liverpool accent). Before coming over I did not know that not everyone spoke the Queen's English. It was an interesting discovery to find out that there were so many different accents in England and across the whole UK.

Mum and I were finally living in a spacious, two-bedroom flat in a very nice area in Bedfordshire. This was our fourth accommodation since I had arrived in England, and I loved it. It was quite close to the town centre but also in a quiet residential area. Before that, I had experienced all the different types of living accommodations one could experience. We lived in a shared flat for about a month before we moved to a studio flat. Though at the time I was just grateful that we no longer had to share our cooking and bathroom space with anyone else, we could not stay there as it was so draughty. We were not there long before we also noticed that there was a lot of mould in the studio. We realized this was the reason it was cheaper than the other places Mum had viewed. She thought she had got a bargain. It appeared the owners had not addressed the underlying issue; instead, they had just put on a fresh coat of paint to disguise what was underneath. It was a lesson in how someone could dress up nicely and look good on the outside, but their heart could be bad.

A few weeks after that, we had to move again. This time it was to a one-bedroom flat with separate kitchen, living area, and bedroom. It was not a problem that I was still sharing a bedroom with my mum. It was a new build, so it was very clean with no mould or draught. After we had been there for a year, my late stepfather's estate was finally sorted and we could now afford to live in a spacious two-bedroom apartment. Finally, I could have my own bedroom with my own bed. I felt settled.

My two-year working visa was coming to an end. I had decided that I wanted to do something more, and the only way I could do that was to go back to school and get the kind of qualifications that would be recognised in UK. I had done an access course at one of the local colleges, so now I had the qualifications to go to university as a mature student.

Whilst a few people told me that, because I already had a degree from Sierra Leone, I could apply to do my master's, I had no idea what I should be doing my master's in. I did not want to continue with Linguistics or Religious Studies; I wanted to do something different, something that would get me into a corporate environment. I had done well in A Level Economics whilst I was in sixth form, but I had not gotten good enough grades in Mathematics at O Levels to get me into the business field at university. But now with my new access, I could get into the business field. I was very much interested in Marketing.

Everything was looking good; I was now at university. I was looking forward to what the future might hold after I completed my marketing degree in three years at the University of Bedfordshire (previously known as the University of Luton).

Sometimes it may seem as if everything is going well, then suddenly it is not. What you least expect happens, and life as you know it changes. Then things are never the same as before. Don't get me wrong; whilst some events are life changing, they also shape you into the person that you need to be for your next step. At the time you are going through a life-changing event, you are not aware that you are developing attributes that will make you a better person. We prepare to take tests and exams at school that will show we are ready for the next step in our education, or we finish a project or secondment at work to show that we are ready for the next step in a career. It is similar in life: we go through trials and tests, and when we come through, we look back and see that our character has developed. We have more patience or endurance than before.

I never expected that life would change drastically in my fifth year of living in England. My faith in God was strong. I was very much involved in the youth and women's ministry at my local church. God had created opportunities for me to share His Word on a number of occasions. I had been pleasantly surprised that God could use me as a communicator in our church. I was also leading Sunday school for some of the youth.

In the summer before I started university, I noticed my mum was complaining about being constipated and not having regular bowel movements as she should. She did not think it was anything serious, so she took laxatives and ate more fruits and other food that would help give her regular bowel movements. After some weeks she had not said anything more about it, so I thought all was well. Unbeknown to me, she had made an appointment with her doctor, and the doctor had referred her to the hospital to see a consultant. She had already seen the consultant, who had done some tests without my knowing.

The first I found out about this development was when she got a call from the consultant to give her the results of the test and she was told that she should attend the consultation with someone else. Mum had no other choice but to tell me that she had been concerned enough with the continuous constipation that she had seen her doctor. He had then referred her to the hospital, and she needed me to go with her for another appointment with the consultant. Although I was shocked that she had kept all of this to herself, it was not surprising. Mum was a very private person and would only share personal things if she had no other choice. I trusted God that all would be well. I knew what my mum was like. She had been like that all her life, and I did not expect her to change in her later years. I was glad the consultant had asked her to bring someone, as this meant I could ask all the questions and would get all the information we needed.

I was not prepared for what the consultant told us once we got to his office at the hospital. We were both unprepared for it. It was like having a flashback to when I was eleven years old, but worse.

Back in Sierra Leone, my mum had had a big celebration for her fiftieth birthday, which was unlike her, as she was otherwise very conservative. After the party she started experiencing severe constipation. Not only was she having constipation, but she was also losing weight rapidly and her stomach was protruding as if she were pregnant. I was eleven years old at the time and actually thought that I was getting another sibling; I always equated a protruding stomach with a baby. Shortly after this, my eldest brother (whom I had never met because I was born after he had left for Germany to study medicine) made arrangements for Mum to travel to Germany to have an operation. He was now a qualified doctor and was practising at the hospital where Mum would be admitted. Mum had a tumour in her stomach, which is why she was unwell. I did not know any of this until much later. At the time, I was just told that she was unwell and that the treatment she needed could only be done overseas. That was my first indication that Sierra Leone's health care system was inadequate, if people had to leave Sierra Leone to get medical help.

She was successfully treated in Germany and stayed there for about six months under the care of my brother. She had to recuperate thoroughly before she could be signed off from the hospital. She came back home with a scar that was the whole length of her stomach. She would share with us how long the operation was and all the details of the care she had to get afterward. Thankfully she had been told that the tumour was benign.

Here we were almost twenty years later, being told that the tumour was back, but this time it was not benign. The test result from the biopsy had shown it was cancer. That six-letter word that no one wants to hear. Being a believer, I was hopeful. I thought, *We are no longer in Sierra Leone; we are in England where there is a more than adequate health care system.* She would be fine. She had defeated this tumour before and she would defeat it again. I tuned out the conversation for a few seconds as my mind wandered off. I was jolted back to the present when I heard the word "spread." I had to ask the consultant to recap what he had said. He said, "I am sorry, but the cancer has spread." It was now inoperable, which meant it was terminal. Mum started crying. This strong woman whom I had known all my life, who held in her emotions in public, really fell apart in that consultation room after hearing the news that the cancer was inoperable. I was devastated. As the news sunk in, I also started crying. I forgot that I was supposed to be there to comfort her. But honestly I don't know who was comforting who, as we were both crying in front of the consultant. He gave us some tissues and time to calm our emotions before he told us the next steps. Next steps involved chemo and radiotherapy to extend her life for a few months. Basically, we were being told that mum had less than a year to live.

How could this be? Why would this happen just when we were finally settled? I was just about to start university. I had successfully been given a grant for the fees; even though in those days going to university was free for citizens, because I was not a citizen, I had to pay. But as I had been living in the county for the last three years, I was not technically considered a foreign student. I received an exemption from the fees that foreign students who had only just arrived would have had to pay.

In those early days I could not get my head around the news that I was going to lose my mum. This would be different from losing Frank, as the grieving process started as soon as I heard the words "cancer" and "inoperable." It was as if the consultant had told me that Mum was dead. Neither of us could believe it. It was hard to plan for the future knowing that Mum would not be with me for much longer.

Mum was constantly crying when it was just the two of us. This made me really sad. Over time I realised that it was normal that your parents pass before you, so I had to be strong for her.

In the midst of my grief, I also had this irrational anger directed at my mum or God, I was not sure at the time. I felt that I had only had a short time with my mum. *If only she had had me when she was younger* was one of my selfish thoughts. Then we would have had longer together. She would have lived to see my children, her grandchildren. I would cry, "Lord, why was I not born when my mum was in her thirties so we could have had longer?" It was irrational when I thought about it later, but at the time I needed to release my emotions. This anger against my mum and against God seemed relevant to me.

8

Surprises and Challenges

It was only a few months before that that we had celebrated Mum's seventieth birthday. It had been a very quiet one since she did not want any fuss. As we approached the big day, I had asked her what she wanted to do and had suggested a party, which she immediately declined. She told me she wanted it to just be us: me, her, my adopted sister, Sophia and her family (there were now four of them), and Frank's daughter who would be coming up from London with her mum.

I discussed with my sister-in-law, my cousin Sophia, and my adopted sister who lived in Hounslow how I wanted to hold a small surprise party for Mum's seventieth birthday. They all agreed that it would be great to do something to celebrate this significant milestone. Together with close family and friends, we planned the day. A close friend of hers from another church took her out for the morning whilst, together with a few helpers, I put up banners and balloons. We had also got a cake, as no birthday party would be complete without a birthday cake and candles. I had deliberated on whether or not to have balloons with her age on them; Mum was very particular about whom she shared personal details with, especially her age. But I did not think she would mind, as these were all people who were very close to her who would know how old she was anyway.

She was pleasantly surprised when she arrived home with her friend who had kept her occupied whilst we decorated the flat. There were less than twelve people there, all very close family and friends with whom she was happy to share her birthday. We had cooked our traditional food, jollof rice with chicken stew, and made the usual drinks, homemade ginger beer. As a Sierra Leonean from the Krio ethnic group, there was no way you could have a celebration without jollof rice and homemade ginger beer. Although she had said she did not want a fuss, she really enjoyed the low-key celebration. We spent time reminiscing about Sierra Leone, we took photos for the memory book, and we made a lot of phone calls home. We did not realize at the time how significant this celebration was. I am always telling people to enjoy and treasure the present moment with loved ones, because we do not know what might happen tomorrow. Tomorrow is not guaranteed.

We never knew that this would be her last birthday with us. Just a few months later we received the appalling diagnosis that she had terminal cancer and had less than a year to live. She had to start chemotherapy immediately to reduce the speed at which the cancer was spreading. She would have to have the chemo at the Mount Vernon hospital, but it was not close to us. Because she did not want many people to know what was going on, we had to depend on transportation provided by the local authority. At this time only our pastor and his wife were aware of her diagnosis. She had sworn me to secrecy. I was not to tell any of the family in Sierra Leone that she had cancer. She would tell them when she was ready.

To prepare her for the chemotherapy sessions, we had to visit the hospital in Mount Vernon before she actually started the treatment. The nurse who was supporting us told us it would be good for her to take up this offer so that she would know exactly what was happening and where. We went down the week before she started the chemo. It seemed like a long journey from where we lived, even though it was less than an hour's drive. When we arrived, we were shown the room where the chemo would be done and also told how long it would take. Mum and I definitely did not like the smell of the anaesthetic, the usual hospital smell of sickness and death. It was good to make this visit, but it also brought home the reality of Mum's illness. Soon she would look like some of the patients we saw whilst we were being shown around. People with no hair, people looking sick and being sick. On the journey back home, we were both very quiet. The visit had confirmed that there were some tough days ahead.

Before the diagnosis she had discussed observing the upcoming fifth anniversary of Frank's passing with my sister-in-law. She was not going to let the cancer diagnosis stop her. She started making preparation for my brother's anniversary memorial. In October of that year, it would be five years since we lost Frank. I went along with it, as it gave her something to take her mind off her predicament. Together with our pastor and his wife, we were believing God for a miracle. I was holding on to the verses in the Bible where it says

"Who has believed [confidently trusted in, relied on, and adhered to] our message [of salvation]? And to whom [if not us] has the arm *and* infinite power of the Lord been revealed?" (Isaiah 53:1)

The gospel song from Ron Kenoly was also very popular around this time: "Whose report will you believe?" / "We shall believe the report of the Lord."

I was definitely choosing to believe the report of the Lord, not what the report from the consultant had said. I believed that Mum would live beyond the time frame given by the report. Don't get me wrong; I do believe in science and all that the medical world has to offer. But I also believe that the brains and knowledge that they have, they received from God. Therefore, God has the final say. So, I would listen to the doctors, trusting that God could guide them to administer the right treatment. But I also believe that only God knows when we will leave this earth. No matter what the medical people said, I would always look to God for His direction. He has the final say.

I remember how sick Mum was after the first chemo session. I wondered how something that made her feel so sick could be any good for her. For a few days after the session, she would throw up a lot. She would be very sick before she would start to feel better. I cannot remember how many sessions she had during that summer. She still had not yet shared with family in Sierra Leone how sick she was. On the outside she looked the same, so no one could tell that something was wrong when she was not throwing up. If she was feeling better, she would go to church with me. It was around this time that I met Trevor.

One of my mum's biggest fears about her diagnosis was that I was the only one of her children in England whilst all her other children were in Sierra Leone. My three older brothers, including the one who qualified as a doctor in Germany, were now in Sierra Leone. She kept thinking about her imminent death and how I would be left on my own with none of my siblings nearby. I caught her crying a few times when she thought I was still out, and I knew immediately that's what she was thinking. She admitted it on one such occasion. She would have me in tears, because I knew she would not be here when I met someone, got married, and had children. Though she had grandchildren from my older brothers, she had been praying ever since I had come to England to live with her that I would meet someone who I would eventually marry.

I first met Trevor at a barbecue that I did not want to go to. I had just come home from my part-time job at one of the shops in the mall. I was tired, but I had promised my friend Jacqueline that I would cook some jollof rice for her nephew's first birthday party. The celebration was a barbecue at her cousin's house, and I had to keep my word. Mum was over the moon when I told her later that weekend that I had met someone, and that he wanted to meet with her.

In the weeks that followed, she got to know Trevor very well. It's as if we had known Trevor for much more than just a few weeks. Mum felt comfortable with him and would call him if she needed something. It was strange that she did not hesitate to share with him—someone who had just come into our lives—that she was not well, whilst her sisters and children in Sierra Leone had no idea about the magnitude of her illness. She would reach out to Trevor if she had the craving to eat certain food, and Trevor would get it for her since he had a car and could easily pick up things that she needed. Trevor was so good with my mum. He embraced her as if they had known each other for years and not just a few months. Mum told him about her plans for the five-year anniversary memorial for my brother and extended an invitation for him to attend. He accepted.

For someone who was not familiar with our food and traditions, he was amazing. I had thought that he might not come because he was a bit of an introvert and this was a biggie. There were family and friends from London who had come for the memorial cook-up. He had previously met my cousin Sophia but not any other family members. He would be coming on his own and meeting all these people for the first time, most of whom are from Sierra Leone and would be speaking our native dialect Krio. Honestly I did not think he would make it. But then he really surprised me. He came and did not hesitate to sit on the carpet after we had run out of enough chairs with so many people in the flat. He felt right at home and fit right in with our family and friends. I did not know at the time that he was out of his comfort zone, though over the years of being married to him, I realized how he had pushed through his discomfort to be there. He ate all the food offered to him even though this was the first time he was trying some of the different dishes. This made mum very happy. I was quite pleased as well, as it indicated that we would get on.

9

First and Last Christmas

As we approached Christmas 1997, it became obvious to everyone that Mum was not well. She had lost a lot of weight. Previous Christmases she and I had spent the day with my cousin Sophia and her family. We would visit her church then have Christmas dinner with them all afterward. But since this was the first Christmas after meeting Trevor, we decided to do something different. Mum was not up to visiting anyone, so Trevor came to our home first to spend some time with Mum and me. Then he and I went off to Sophia's and later to his parents' house. All his sisters and his brother would be there with their partners, along with lots of visiting nieces and aunties and cousins. It was a great time for me to meet the close family, as I had already met his parents.

It was a really bittersweet time for me. I had Trevor in my life and things were going well with us and this was our first Christmas together. But even though I was trusting God for Mum to be healed, I was also thinking this could be our last Christmas together. It was hard. How could I enjoy my first Christmas with Trevor when this could be my last Christmas with Mum? At this time, she still had not told the family in Sierra Leone about her cancer, and it was weighing heavily on me. At that time the rebel war was in full force in Sierra Leone and all international flights had been suspended. When we had calls from my aunts and my brothers, she would put on a brave front and would speak in a very cheerful voice so that none of them were any the wiser.

At the start of 1998, she was now on radiotherapy. This was really putting a strain on her immune system, so I encouraged her once again to tell her sisters, starting with my aunt who had brought me over to England. I made the call, and Mum told her sister. They decided not to tell their mum, my grandmother, as she was very old and would have been very upset. She had been very upset when Frank passed. I made the call to my brothers, and they were all devastated, especially when I told them the cancer had spread and it was terminal. It was a really sad day for us. At this time most of the church family knew, as Mum was not going to church anymore. The pastor's wife whom she was close with would visit her and share the Bible with her. She would also put on some of the gospel songs we sang in church so that spiritually she was still being fed. We also had lots of video and tape recordings of our church services that she could listen to.

I had thought the chemo sessions were bad, but the radiotherapy sessions were even worse. They left her really sick. The radiation made her incontinent, so she had to use surgical pads. She was becoming really skinny. Sometimes I would look at her and could not recognise this woman who used to be very voluptuous with a great figure. She had become skin and bones, and it was heartbreaking. With tears she would tell me about what she wanted for her funeral service, and I was of two minds. I did not want to talk about it, but yet I needed to know what her final wishes were. It was devastating. She had already spoken to a close family friend in Houston, Texas, who would send the dress she wanted me to lay her in. It was so sad. When the dress arrived, I took it out of the packaging so she could see what it looked like, and she loved it. There were parts of this that were surreal for me, as I could not believe that my mum would not be here to see me finish university, get married, or have children.

Because she knew she would not be here to see my children, she would talk to me about how I should not forget our customs and upbringing. She would tell me that some of us who were born in Sierra Leone or in other African countries forget our upbringing and would bring up our children according to Western ways. She would go on about respecting elders and letting children being children without allowing the child to rule the home. I don't know what her reference point was, but she was keen on driving into me that I must ensure my future children would be respectful and know how to address elders. They were not to address people who could be their parents by their first names. I was also to make sure that they would not take things for granted and that they would start doing little chores when they were small. She kept quoting from this verse in the Bible:

"Train up a child in the way he should go [teaching him to seek God's wisdom and will for his abilities and talents], Even when he is old he will not depart from it" (Proverbs 22:6).

"If you start when they are small, showing them what is right from wrong and letting them know they will not get away with bad behaviour, then it will be easier when they are older," she said. As I said before, even though I was the daughter she had longed for, Mum never let me off easily if I had behaved badly or done something wrong. There was no way I would bring up my own children in a different way. I would reassure her time and again that I would remember what she had said—and that I would not just remember it but would do what she had been drilling into me.

I was still going to university, holding down two part-time jobs, and looking after Mum during this time. When I think back on what I went through, I know that it could only be God who saw me through. He knew how hard the coming days were going to be, so He brought Trevor into my life at the right time. If I needed to go anywhere, he would take me. He would pick me up from the shop in the mall after my late shifts, especially during winter when the evenings got dark early, and then he would drop me off at home. Whilst I was doing my part-time hours in the evening, if Mum needed anything, he would get it for her. I felt really supported by him. My mum had indicated that she would like to have a private conversation with him one day when he came round to visit. After they had the conversation, which I was not part of, I noticed that Mum seemed a bit more relaxed. To this day Trevor has not shared with me what Mum said to him in that private conversation a few months before she passed.

As the cancer was progressing and she was on very strong drugs, she would get very sleepy. It was around this time that I started receiving outside support from the MacMillan Cancer Support nurses as well as from two sisters from church. Mum, being the private person that she was, only wanted a few people to be with her if I had to be away. My friend Jacqueline was one of them along with another older sister from church.

It was very difficult for me when I went to church, as everyone wanted to know how Mum was. I would be repeating the same thing over and over again to five, six, or seven different people, and it became very exhausting. I would have preferred if some people apart from just the pastor and his wife would have called during the week to find out how Mum was, instead of waiting until I was in church on Sunday. I started going to church just in time for the service to start and then leaving before the closing prayer. I could not take it anymore. It was so hard to be repeating the same thing over and over again. In those days there was no WhatsApp, and mobile phones were not as common as they are now. It would have been easier to have a WhatsApp group in which I could update everyone who needed to know the latest about Mum.

The Macmillan nurses were visiting us regularly, and they had been talking to Mum about going to a local hospice for a night or two to give me respite. They told her that the change of scenery would also be good for her. It took a lot of convincing for her to agree to try it. She was very reluctant to do it, mainly because she was now very skinny and had a fear of passing away while she was outside her home. Whereas I preferred for her to be in the hospice when she passed; it would have been too much for me to handle if I was all by myself. I told her to try it for one day and if she did not like it, she would not need to go again. She did it, and all went well. I would not say that she loved it, but when she went, she met other people in the same situation as her and I thought it helped her. She did not feel so alone in this sickness. With the help of the nurses at the hospice, she also spent time crafting a lovely tray that featured a beautiful picture of flowers. She was so proud of herself for making it. When I visited her, she showed it off to Trevor and me. I remember holding the tray and thinking *this will be with me forever*. My mum had always been great with her hands, and until her dying days, she was using her talent to make something that would be part of her legacy. I have kept it and use it even to this day.

10

Saying Good-bye to Mum

Mum was now much weaker and often very sleepy, as the drugs were increased to reduce her pain and discomfort. She was spending more time at the local hospice, and I was slowly beginning to accept that any time now I would get a call informing me that she had passed. It was really hard for me. After she finally told my aunt in Sierra Leone, she also gave her permission to inform the other aunties in London. The auntie who we had stayed with when I first arrived in England told me that she wanted to visit her. I was not too sure whether Mum would be open to the idea of a visit. To my surprise she agreed. My auntie came from London with two of her sisters to see Mum at the hospice. One of them had been my mum's bridesmaid when she had gotten married, so they were really upset. She asked me why I had not said anything earlier. I could only tell her that Mum did not want a fuss and had not wanted anyone to know. To a certain extent they understood, but I could sense that they were not happy that they had only been informed when she was more or less on her last days. I could also understand things from my mum's perspective, given that, even when she was healthy, it was not as if we had regularly visited our family in London or vice versa.

It is very important that, when everything is going well, we show love and care to those that are dear to us. We should not wait until they are sick or on their deathbed. Most people only want close people around them when they are on their deathbed. They are usually vulnerable and not looking their best, so there is always a fear that anyone who comes close to them when they are in that state are only doing so with ulterior motives. In some cases, this is true. When you are in that phase of illness, the person who is sick wants to have some amount of control over the narrative. You do not want people exaggerating how bad you look just to tell a "good sad" story. The only way to accomplish this is, usually, to limit the amount of people who visit you during that phase. Not that my aunties were people who would do something like that, but Mum was very cautious. She did not agree to visits from many people.

Nowadays there are more treatments available, and recovering from cancer has a higher rate than twenty-six years ago. Even so I do come across people who still want to keep it quiet and only inform a few close people that they are getting treatment for cancer. I think it's because most people associate cancer with death, so once you got it, there was this belief that you would not recover. I think people want to avoid being pitied by others. If the person who is sick is trusting God for healing, telling the wrong person could bring all kinds of unconscious negativity. People might want to tell you about someone else they knew who died of cancer. If it is same type of cancer that the sick person is suffering from, this is not helpful to the sick person's ability to believe in and trust God for a miracle.

When my brother was sick in hospital, it had been unexpected. I had always thought that he died too soon. But in the situation with my mum, I was a little bit more accepting of her forthcoming passing. Still, it did not happen overnight. When I think back on it, I think it's because we had celebrated her seventieth birthday and in the Bible it does say,

"The days of our life are seventy years—Or even, if because of strength, eighty years; Yet their pride [in additional years] is only labour and sorrow, For it is soon gone and we fly away" (Psalm 90:10).

I was trusting God for a miracle, but at the same time trusting that He knows best. My sadness was more selfish, as I thought about all the things that she would miss concerning me. I was in my first year at university, and I thought she would not be here to see me complete my schooling and graduate. She would not see any children that God would bless me with. I had seen how she had taken care of her grandchildren from my brothers, and I was sad that she would not be here for mine.

Her passing was peaceful. I had gone there the evening before, and she was sleeping. I stayed with her for a while, watching her, with tears in my eyes, breathe in and out, wondering if this would be the last time I saw her breathing. It was really sad. Trevor was also with me, and over the last few months, I could see that, even though he had not known my mum for long, she had definitely made an impact on him. He kept telling me that he could not believe how the sickness had progressed so quickly. He could not stay in the room. He had to wait for me outside in the car because it made him too emotional seeing my mum like that. As much as I hated being there, because all around me I saw other patients in different stages of passing from this life in such a very depressing scene, I could not stay away. When I was ready to leave, I took her hands in mine and told her that I loved her. What else could I say, apart from letting her know that she was loved and that I promised

I would remember all the advice she had given me and the wisdom she had passed to me over the years.

Early the next morning, which was a Thursday, I got a call from the hospice, and I immediately knew that Mum had passed. I was not surprised when they told me that she had passed early that morning; one of the nurses had been with her at the time. She said I could come to the hospice to collect her things, and if the death certificate was ready, I could take it to the registration office. I felt alone even though I knew I was not alone. I had lovely people around me who were supporting me, but they were not my mum. It was really hard. Even years later, I still miss her. There is a bond between a mother and her child that is very strong. The bond between mum and I had been very strong indeed.

I recalled three other occasions when I had been apart from my mum. The first was when I was about five years old and she had left us to further her studies in England. She was away for two years, and all I could remember from those days was how sad I was. The aunt who I was staying with only had to call me by name and I would start crying because I was missing my mum so much. When she returned from England and we were all back together, it was such a relief. She had missed us also and vowed that she would not leave us behind the next time she had to go away. The next time we were apart was when I was about eleven years old and she had to go to Germany for the operation to remove the tumour in her stomach. She was gone for about six months and again it was hard. The third time was when she came over to England whilst I was in my early twenties, and we were separated for just over a year before I joined her there. It does not matter who else you have in your life; they could be a lovely person, a mother figure, but they can never replace your birth mother once you have developed that bond together.

And I was now experiencing the separation that was final on this earth. I did believe that we would meet again, but it would be in another place, not here on earth, so it was really hard.

When I went to the hospice to collect her stuff, it was with mixed feelings. I was relieved that I would not have to come to the hospice again to see my mum in the condition that really depressed me. This was not because she was not taken care of at the hospice—quite the opposite. She was pampered and looked after very well. The depressing thing for me is that it was where she lost more weight and became almost skin and bones. It was where I saw her confined to a bed, not able to sit on a chair anymore. It was where I saw her drifting in and out of consciousness, barely able to acknowledge that I was there. It was the place where every day someone else who I'd gotten used to seeing would be gone by the next time I visited, which reminded me that soon that would be Mum, here today but gone tomorrow. So yes, I was relieved, but with that relief came the sadness that I was there for the last time to collect her belongings as well as the death certificate. The death certificate was a symbol of finality. A person who was so full of life is gone. No more would you see them laughing or hear the sound of their voice. It was the end. They had passed from this life. It was really hard.

I trusted God to be my father and mother as he promised in the Bible:

"A father of the fatherless and a judge *and* protector of the widows, is God in His holy habitation" (Psalm 68:5).

I was fatherless and now motherless. God would look after me. I trusted Him to give me the strength because He cares for me. He knows exactly how much I can take and will not give me more than I can bear. This He says in these verses in the Bible:

"No temptation [regardless of its source] has overtaken or enticed you that is not common to human experience [nor is any temptation unusual or beyond human resistance]; but God is faithful [to His word—He is compassionate and trustworthy], and He will not let you be tempted beyond [to resist], but with the temptation He [has in the past and is now and] will [always] provide the way out as well, so that you will be able to endure it [without yielding, and will overcome temptation with joy]" (1 Corinthians 10:13).

God knew exactly how much I could take; He knows how strong I am and how weak I am at the same time. Some people get a diagnosis and the time until their passing could be short; sometimes it could take weeks. God knew that I was not strong enough at that time to cope with a sudden death like my brother's passing. So, in this situation, I had months to prepare myself and learn to accept it, to get stronger emotionally so that I could bear it when Mum passed. The above verse is definitely true in my situation; I needed time before she passed to adjust to what life would be like without Mum.

11

Planning Mum's Service

I had never been involved in planning a funeral before, and I did not know where to start. I had only been living in England for five years, so I still did not know how to navigate such things. The Macmillan nurses and the staff at the hospice were really great in supporting me. They gave me a list of the local funeral services and walked me through what the process would be. Three of my close friends who had also been close to my mum came to spend some time with me. My cousin Sophia who lived locally was also there to support me. And of course, Trevor took time off to be our chauffeur, driving us everywhere we needed to go to put the plans in motion for the funeral.

At least I did not have to think about what Mum would wear, as this had already been decided before she passed. I only had to hand it over to the funeral home. I had to speak to my pastor and his wife regarding the date of the funeral service and where we could have the service. We did not have a building of our own for a worship service, as we used to hire one of the meeting rooms in the town hall and we could not use this for the service. We were affiliated with one of the local churches, which was a Church of

England, and we were quite familiar with the vicar there. It was decided that this would be a fitting venue to hold the service.

With the help of family and friends who knew Mum very well, we put together the hymns and songs that she would have liked. I knew one or two that she had always been humming or singing since we were children, so both those and a few more contemporary songs she had grown to love were added. When we were talking about her impending passing, we had not gone into details about what songs and hymns she wanted for her funeral. At that point I would not have been able to bear it. Though she was emphatic that she did not want to be taken home to Sierra Leone for burial. That and what she would wear were the things that she had been very clear about.

Once I had decided which funeral home we would use, we had to have a meeting to choose the coffin. It is such a daunting experience, especially when you are doing it for the first time. I had hoped that my aunt who had first brought me over would be able to come to England for the funeral so I could have an older family member, and someone who was also close to Mum, to support me. I thought I needed someone that I could lean on. Unfortunately during this time, the airport was still closed to international flights as the rebel war was still raging on. I could only lean on God. There were no close family members apart from my cousins, aunties from London, and close family friends in attendance. All of this was quite new for Trevor also, so he could only support me by being available to take me where we needed to go. Since the planning did involve a lot of driving, I was grateful that God had brought him into my life when He did.

Eight days later, we had the funeral for Mum. It was a Friday. I had agreed with the funeral directors that we wanted her to be brought to the house where the coffin would be opened for viewing, as this was our custom. I needed to do video recordings for the family in Sierra Leone, since, as I said, they were not able to come over due to the war there. Whilst it would likely not be easy viewing for them, the least I could do was give them the choice of watching the recording or not, which I would send to them at a later date. If I had not recorded it, I would have taken that choice away from them. There was a lovely brother in church who had kindly offered to do the recording, as he videotaped most of our Sunday services and special events. Luckily that was now something else that I did not have to think about.

We had not thought too clearly about the logistics of getting the coffin into our two-bedroom flat. Although we lived on the ground floor, it proved to be a challenge. I am sure the funeral directors later made sure to amend their consultation pack by adding the question, "Could we visit the home before bringing the coffin there on the day?" But they made it work, so anyone who had not seen Mum for a while had the choice of coming to the house an hour before the service to see her laid out in the lovely dress she had requested from our family friend in America. She looked very peaceful in the coffin. She did not look like the skin and bones she had been in the last week before she passed.

Mum had also requested that we would not wear black to her funeral. She had told me that she would prefer if we wore white. This is mainly for the women; the men were not expected to wear white. It is the custom in Sierra Leone, and definitely for the Krio ethnic group who we belong to, to always choose a colour, and on some occasions even choose the fabric, that the close family will wear as a sign of togetherness and identification. I did not want to do that, so I chose a two-piece white suit for myself and for my adopted sister. I did inform all the female friends and relations that we would wear white. I also chose black hats to wear with the outfit.

I was going through the motions, as I was all cried out. I was in the midst of people who loved me but still felt as if I were on my own. I can only put that feeling down to the fact that no other person, no friend or family member, could share in the emotions that I was feeling, because they were unique to me. My relationship with my mum, being the only daughter she had, was unique to me and her, and that caused the aloneness. I remember walking behind the coffin as it was carried into the church, and it felt as if it were not me. For some reason I thought, *If this was really mum's funeral, my brothers would be here.* I would not be doing this on my own. I would not have to make all the decisions, without knowing if I was making the right ones. So yes, I was going through the motions with a heavy heart. There was also a part of me that was disappointed with my aunt because she did not come over. I thought if anyone could have come, it would have been her, as she had the means. I knew I was being unreasonable, but I could not help it. I had even offered to pay for the ticket, as family and friends from both near and far had been very generous in giving monetary gifts towards the funeral planning. For some time afterward I held it against her that she did not make it for the funeral. It took me a while to forgive her for not coming. Not that she could have come, but in my grief I was not considering all the challenges and obstacles that prevented her travelling to England.

The service was lovely just as Mum would have wanted. There were quite a lot of people there, including Trevor's sister and her husband. I was really touched, as they had not even met my mum, but they had heard a lot about her from Trevor. There was also family from London who attended the funeral. Afterward, we had a repast at a local restaurant. The whole day was a bit of a blur for me. It was a very sad and emotional event, and emotionally exhausting for me.

Since Mum had not wanted to be taken back to Sierra Leone, I had paid for her to be buried in a plot at the local cemetery. She had said at the time that, since I had met Trevor, she saw my future to be in England, not in Sierra Leone. So, she wanted to be buried here, where I would always be near to her place of rest and able to visit and lay flowers on her grave. I agreed with her, as at that time it would have been a very serious logistic issue to take her body to Sierra Leone.

After the funeral I had to navigate a new normal without my mum. I could not stay in the flat, as there were too many memories, both good and bad, which were making me really sad. Also, without her income I could not afford to keep it on my own. I had decided I would look for a one-bedroom flat or studio that I could afford with the salary from the two part-time jobs I had. I was still at university and could not work full time even if I wanted to, as I was on a student's visa.

Fortunately, it was easy to find another flat that would be suitable for me. It was still very close to the town centre and all the places I frequented. I was able to put down a deposit, give notice to the landlord of the flat we had been renting, and then get back the deposit Mum had put down, which came in handy. It was quite an emotional experience packing up to move out of the flat. Mum had acquired a lot of stuff before she became ill. There were things she had planned to ship over to Sierra Leone for my brothers and her grandchildren. I had no clue that she had so much stuff, including clothes, shoes, household items, and educational material. I could have opened a bric-a-brac shop with all the stuff I had to put into storage, as I could not bear to give it away at that time. There was no way I could move everything we had in the two-bedroom flat into a one-bedroom flat. Trevor suggested storing some of the stuff that I did not need immediately at his parents' house, as they had an outside shed with space for storage. I was grateful for this alternative.

My new place was in a shared house but was self-contained with my own kitchen and bathroom. I only shared the main entrance into the house. It was a massive house that had been converted into self-contained flats, and it suited my needs. It was also less than ten minutes' walk from the flat where Mum and I had lived. I was fortunate to have found it, as I did not have to change my route to work or to the university. It was the same route, just from a different starting point.

I loved my flat. It was the first time I had ever had a place of my own. I had always lived with someone, so it was great to experience being fully independent. I was in my early thirties and this was the first time I was living on my own. I could decorate and furnish the place the way I liked it, according to my own taste. My mum loved little ornaments and stuff. I did not mind them, but I wanted my space to be a bit minimalistic, not too crowded. It was great to be able to put my stamp on the place and show my personality.

I was not there for long. This was my new home for only six months, as Trevor and I got married exactly six months after my mum passed. I had not seen that in my immediate future, but God works in mysterious ways.

12

Different Losses: How Do They Compare?

The loss of my mum was very hard, as I missed her terribly. We had been a unit since I had arrived in England. The loss I felt was different from the loss of my brother Frank. The pain was different and the healing was different. This is something very important for those who have never experienced loss of a close loved one before to know. If you are supporting a person who has lost someone dear to them, don't make comparisons between experiences. All deaths are experienced differently. The journey and pace will be different.

When I lost my brother, I experienced very different emotions compared to what I experienced when I lost my mum. I felt alone when I lost mum because my brothers and other close family were in Sierra Leone. When I lost my brother, I was in Sierra Leone with my other brothers and close family, but Mum was in England, so the emotions were different.

I lost my dad before I lost my brother and my mum. I would say that was the first significant loss I experienced before my brother.

The difficulty in that loss was that I felt I had not gotten to know him as well as I could have. My mum and dad were not married, so I never got to know my dad as well as I would have liked because I never lived with him.

The short visits with my dad at his house were very superficial in a way. I was always on my best behaviour, so he did not get to see the real me. He was very much old-school, very focused on education. He put a lot of emphasis on working hard at school and university to attain good results. He drilled into my brother and me that that was all he could give us, a good education. But no one could take that away from us. I don't disagree with him, but I also think that part of an education is also being taught important life skills. These I had to depend on my mum for.

I got to know my dad a bit more when I was able to visit him in his office. If I was showing him good results from school, it would put him in a good mood. Then we could chat about other stuff; it wouldn't just be him scolding me like he did if I brought bad results from school. I also felt in those days that my visits were always centred around something I needed, rather than visiting him simply because he was my dad. At the time it seemed to me like a waste to spend all that money on transportation if I was not also combining the effort with a request for something I needed for school or for home. When I reflect on it now, I do feel bad. But unfortunately, as a child with parents living in two different locations, I had to make it work.

My last few visits to him had been because I had been chosen by one of my cousins to be one of the chief bridesmaids at her wedding. I was really excited, as it was the first time I had been asked, so it would be my first time as part of a bridal party. I needed shoes and fabric to make the dress. In those days people hardly went to a shop to get ready-made outfits, and I had already learnt how to make dresses from mum, as she was very good with the sewing machine. All I really needed was the fabric to make the outfit for the wedding.

My dad was very interested in the role I would be playing as a chief bridesmaid. We used to discuss what was required and how I would make sure that the bride had a good day. I never thought that he would pass before the wedding took place. But a week or so before the wedding, he was admitted to the hospital for something that at first was minor but then became very serious.

My brother and I visited him at the hospital, as it was walking distance from where we lived. In the short conversation that we had, he quoted *Macbeth*: "If it were done when 'tis done, then 'twere well / It were done quickly" (1.7.1). This is very similar to what Jesus says to Judas in the Bible: "What you are going to do, do quickly [without delay]" (John 13:27). This has stuck with my brother and me all these years, because that was the last thing he said to us before he passed.

The next day when we were informed that he had passed, we could not believe it. Even though we were not very close, it was still hard. With the loss of my dad, I mourned the missed opportunities to get to know him as a person, to learn what he liked apart from his love for good education. I mourned that I did not get to know what his favourite colour or his favourite food were, as my time with him had been so functional. It was mostly about schoolwork, doing well in school to achieve qualifications. He was very disciplined and to some extent, I was always afraid of putting my foot wrong, which meant that I did not get to know him as well as I would have liked.

I remember when I got to puberty and started noticing boys. Mum had caught me reading romances published by Mills & Boon and a Caroline Courtney regency romance book. I had moved on from my Enid Blyton children's books and she was concerned. She told my dad, who thought the best thing would be to get me a book that would educate me on everything a teenage girl should know. He actually bought a book called *Everything a Teenage Girl Should Know*, written by Dr. John F. Knight. I got more than I bargained for with that book. My suggestion to any mums and dads out there is to make sure you have read the book in question before giving it to your children, especially if they are in the early stages of puberty. My mum and dad were very traditional and very uncomfortable talking about the "birds and the bees," so it was either having a stuttering and embarrassing conversation or giving me a book that perhaps said a lot more than they wanted to say.

Though I was not as close to my dad as I was to my mum, his passing was still a great loss to me. As I was much younger at the time, the responsibility of arranging the funeral was left to my dad's siblings and to my own older siblings. They did all the planning, and I just did what I was told, which was mainly going with them to different places as the funeral arrangements came together.

Another loss that I experienced after my mum was my maternal grandmother. I was close with my grandmother, so when I first came to England, she was one of the people I missed a lot. I had spent some of my early years with her when my mum had gone to study in England. For about two years, we lived with my grandmother and my aunt (the one who later brought me to England). In those days she was very strong and would manage the home so that my aunt could focus on being the high-powered obstetrician and gynaecologist that she was. My grandmother used to look after chickens, ducks, and goats, as we were not in the city but in a smaller town outside the capital. At that early age we had the responsibility of feeding the chickens in the morning and evening.

I loved the baby chicks and the baby ducklings, and I remember chasing after the chickens if they escaped from the coop. This is probably one of the reasons I really loved the children's movie *Chicken Run*, which I used to love watching with my children when they were younger.

I had continued to spend a lot of time with my grandmother, even after I was no longer living with her. I would visit her religiously every two weeks to do her hair. She loved having her scalp moisturised, as she said it was like receiving a head massage. She would nod off to sleep, so I would be gentle while doing her hair in order not to wake her up. She also taught me how to mark canvass with wool to make carpet slippers, which was the customary footwear to be worn with a traditional Krio outfit.

It was really sad when she passed, especially as I was in England and could not attend the funeral. But she had lived a long and happy life and died at ninety-five years old.

13

Marley, Always in My Heart

I would like to say that all these different losses I had gone through had prepared me for the hardest loss I was yet to face, but I would be telling a lie. I don't believe that previous losses can prepare you for the next loss you encounter, as all losses are different and, depending on the circumstances, subsequent losses could be even harder to endure than the previous ones. This was the case with my youngest son, who I lost to death by suicide. If you don't know the background to this story, then I recommend reading my book *Marley's Memoir: The Journey to an Irreversible Action and the Aftermath*.

It is now coming up on four years since I lost my youngest son Marley just a week after his eighteenth birthday. Some days it feels like yesterday. On other days, I feel like it happened longer than four years ago.

I still struggle with meeting new people who don't know my story. I dread when the inevitable questions come up, *Do you have any children? How many children have you got?* But I was really encouraged recently when I met someone in church for the first time who had a six-month-old baby. Even before I could ask her about her baby, she told me she had five children. In my heart I was thinking, *Wow, she must have her hands full*, as I reckoned the oldest would not be more than ten years old. She then went on to say that two of the children were in heaven because they had passed—one was a miscarriage and the other was when they were a baby. But she said she always told people that she has five children, it's just that two of them have gone ahead to heaven. I was amazed at her strength and her perspective. I thought I should not shy away from telling people that I have two sons and one has already gone ahead to heaven.

I still talk to God about Marley, asking if there could have been another way. You would think that, after so much time has passed, I would no longer be asking God these kind of questions. But when I think about it, I do feel that I still need that reassurance from God that there was no other way. God is so faithful; He doesn't chastise me for still asking the same question when the deed has already been done. He shows that He cares. He shows that He loves me by reaffirming that there was no other way. He also reminds me that I will not understand everything in this life.

One of the ways He reassures me is by bringing other young people to my attention, young people whose mental health issues have worsened and have even gone on to harm not just themselves but others as well. These actions cause pain and loss for multiple sets of parents, for the parents of the young person with mental health struggles and for the parents whose loved ones were harmed. I have no way of knowing if this could have been our situation as well. But I think back on Marley's lack of response to talk therapy, and I consider that, from the time he finished school to when he ended his life, his mental health had been deteriorating into paranoia, imagining what people were saying and thinking. I can only guess that it might have worsened to the point where he could have harmed someone else. I have to thank God that it did not get to that point.

Since Marley's passing, the foundation that I set up as his legacy, Marley's Aart Foundation, has been providing funding for art therapy for children with mental health conditions. We started working with a local organisation that supports children with emotional and mental health issues, including trauma and bereavement conditions, and we are now working closely with Marley's secondary school. Since we started funding the art therapy at the school, we have made a difference in the mental well-being of over twenty-five different children. The foundation has given me a purpose, knowing I can make a difference for other children and young people who are struggling with their mental health like Marley was. At a recent meeting with the school, it was rewarding to hear the impact of what we are doing through the foundation. At present the foundation funds two individual art therapy sessions once a week and two group therapy sessions once a week for children ranging in age from eleven to sixteen. Some of the children, especially the eleven-year-olds who are new to the school, have found the new school environment much more challenging than their previous schools, especially if they are naturally introverted. They have the tendency to be anxious and have difficulties in social environments meeting new people and making connections. The art therapy really helped them to express themselves and provide mechanisms to help them navigate this phase. This particular age group, transitioning from primary to secondary school, is very dear to me, as it was at this stage that I started noticing a difference in Marley, which at the time I did not understand. I had at first just put it down to the change of school. Now I strongly believe that the earlier the child gets help, the better the response to the therapy will be. I am also very supportive of the children who are suffering from exam anxiety and feeling the pressure to get good grades in order to take their next step in their education. I was especially happy to hear that a number of girls who had suffered with anxiety and missed a lot of school because of it had eventually pushed through to take their GCSEs after they had had group art therapy. It was rewarding to know that Marley's Aart Foundation has helped even in a small way.

I look to God every day as I trust in His plan for the foundation. I am told all the time how God would enlarge the foundation to be national and even international because it is doing such important work. At this moment I am taking it one step at a time, trusting in God for His guidance. If God wants it to stay as it is, just supporting the children in Bedfordshire, then I am happy to be doing that. If He wants it to grow to become national and international, then He will make a way and a provision for that.

Sometimes I am lost in my own world, thinking about Marley and what he would have been doing if he were here. Eight months ago, on the day before he would have turned twenty-one, we held the third Marley's 8KM Memory Walk, a fundraising event that we have been doing since the first anniversary of his passing. This time we had a higher number of supporters than in any of the previous years. It was a very cold, freezing morning, so I was expecting that some of the people who had said they would do the walk might pull out. But as with the previous year, everyone turned out in record numbers to do the five-mile walk. When we reached the end point, I thanked everyone and shared that the next day would have been Marley's twenty-first birthday.

I was in two minds whether to go to church that day or not. In the end I went. I felt I had to push through, because God is with me. When I got to church, I became overwhelmed with what could have been. I allowed myself to imagine what Marley could have looked like. He was a handsome young man, and I think he would probably have filled out into an adult with facial hair. He was also taller than his brother, and I imagined both of them together. It was hard that I had been denied the experience of seeing them like that because he passed so young. I allowed the tears to fall as I sat in church before the service started. A sister who I regularly pray with came over and put her hands around me. She had been sitting behind me, so she must have been prompted by God. Because my tears were silent, she could not hear me or see me, but I leaned into the comfort she was offering. It was hard that I had been robbed of seeing him at twenty-one. After this I felt better. I realised that it had been a while since I had cried over losing Marley. It's not that I don't want to cry or that I hold it in, far from it. In those early days I cried so much that I think I might have run out of physical tears.

I realised that every milestone would be hard for me. When it comes to the years when he would have been twenty-five, thirty, and so forth, I will probably get very emotional. Later I also realised that it's not just his milestones that get me emotional; I am also affected by other children who were born the same year as or the year after him. Each time I celebrate another young person's twenty-first birthday, it will be bittersweet. I would look at Marley's photos from when he was at eighteen and imagine how he would have looked at twenty-one. Would he still be suffering from mental health issues? Would he have become the animator that he wanted to be? These are all unanswered questions that I will not know the answer to in this life. It will always feel like he passed too soon, even though I am slowly accepting that nothing happens too soon in God's timing. The way I feel today, I don't think I will ever accept it. I will always have those questions, whether it is four years or twenty years later.

When I lost my mum, I thought that, after I got married and after I had Nathan and Marley, I would not miss her with the same intensity that I did previously. How wrong I was. Each milestone in my life would remind me of what it would have been like if Mum had been there—to see my children, for my children to know their grandmother, to observe how loving she would have been with them, probably spoiling them by letting them get away with stuff I would not have allowed. The love I have for my mother is a different kind of love compared to the love I have for Marley, and therefore the grief over their losses has been different. Yet the similarity is that they are not here for any future milestones.

Twenty years after my mum passed, I remember waking up one morning and being gripped by a sudden yearning for her voice and touch. That feeling stayed with me for almost the whole day. By the evening, I was sobbing uncontrollably and Trevor and the children were asking me what was wrong. I was so choked up with emotion, I could barely speak. I was finally able to tell them that I missed my mum. Of course, they could not understand what that felt like, because neither Trevor nor the children had lost anyone so close to them. All they could do was give me a hug. Now I know that, after losing Marley, I will not be surprised if ten or twenty years from now, I will get overwhelmed with emotions as if it had just happened. It is the way we are made. Our God cares and weeps over us when we stray from Him and rejoices when we come back to Him. We are made in His image and likeness, as it says in the Bible:

"So, God created man in His own image, in the image *and* likeness of God He created him; male and female He created them" (Genesis 1:27).

It should not come as a surprise to us that we care so much because we are only imitating God our Father.

14

Final Words

The message from my pastor on 29 December 2020 at the service for my son Marley will always stay with me. He voiced what most of us had been thinking or even saying out aloud: Why do bad things happen? Why did this happen? Why would God allow someone who was so young to end their life? He encouraged us to say we do not know why bad things happen. Especially as believers, we may feel we are expected to have all the answers, but we do not have all the answers. We cannot know and we should not try to give an answer to the question of why bad things happen because there are certain things we would not understand or otherwise have the answers for in this life.

We are never ready to lose a loved one. It does not matter how old they are or how sick they are. We may think we are ready if we have walked the journey with that loved one through their illness. But there is something about parting with someone that nothing can prepare you for. When they finally leave this world and we realise that we will never again be able to speak with and interact with that person as before, the reality hits us. We are filled with insurmountable pain and loss.

It has been the same for everyone close to me that I lost. But of all the losses, the three very significant ones are my brother Frank, my mum, and Marley. My dad and the other brothers and relations I have lost have been painful but not as much as these three for the reasons I have shared in the previous chapters. At the church on that horrible day at the service for my son Marley, my pastor told us that, in each situation, God cares. He said that he knows without a doubt that God cares. He cares what happened to Frank, to my mum, and to Marley. He knew how each of these situations would impact me and my future. He went on to quote the following verse from the Bible:

"The Lord is near to the heartbroken And He saves those who are crushed in spirit (contrite in heart, truly sorry for their sin)" (Psalm 34:18).

When we are heartbroken, we may not feel like or think that God is near, but He is. He is the one who helps us to put one foot in front of the other to take one step and another. If it were not for Him, I would not be here. The pain I felt at losing Marley so unexpectedly and suddenly no one could understand. Only God knows. God cares deeply about what happens to us. He knew exactly what Frank was going through; He knew exactly what my mum was going through; and He knew exactly what Marley was going through. He had compassion for their struggles, and because He cares, He allowed them to leave this world. For us it was very painful parting from them. But for those who have left, they were now without any pain.

Each parting also birthed something new. When I lost my brother, it opened the door for me to travel to a new life in England with my mum. I do not know if my aunt would have been moved to purchase a ticket for me to visit my mum if the loss of my brother had not triggered it.

When I lost my mum, it opened the door for me to get married and start a new chapter in my life as a wife and later as a mother. I am not saying that if my mum had not passed I would not have got married. I had of course already met Trevor before my mum passed. What I am saying is that being on my own and experiencing the character development that took place during that time of loss enabled me to move into another level of maturity that served me during the challenges of marriage.

The passing of my son Marley has also opened a door and taken me to another level of maturity. I had never seen myself being an activist. I was more of an advocate—let someone else take the lead and I would be there to support them. With the founding of Marley's Aart Foundation, I have found myself at the front, leading the way with others supporting me in the background. Yes, I have held positions in my career that enabled me to take the lead in several situations, but at the end of the day, there was always someone in front of me. My manager or my manager's manager would be there to act as a cushion to fall back on. I certainly could not push something through if they were not happy with it. In my current role as founder of Marley's Aart Foundation, I have a very strong team of trustees, but they look to me to lead from the front. The unique vision I was given came to me through the pain I experienced then and still experience now any time I meet someone who would be the same age as Marley. The motivation I have to help support children and young people is unique to me. Not that others, especially the trustees, don't have the same motivation, but theirs is coming from a different place than mine. As a mother who lost her son to suicide, I have this burden to help other children in my own small way through the foundation. If the art therapy that the foundation funds prevent one child from taking their life, then my goal is complete. If a mother who has been through similar trauma of losing their child by suicide is comforted by reading about my experience, or if that mother is comforted to find that God cares not just for me but for each and every one of us, and if that mother discovers that because I could be strong then she can be strong as well, then I am satisfied that I have accomplished something.

As I come to the end of this book series on grief and loss, I would like to share that it has been therapeutic for me to write them. Sometimes I have felt very exposed, as I am capturing my raw emotions for others to read and I am sharing about what I have gone through and I am still going through since losing Marley. But I could not be anything other than my authentic self. Though it has been therapeutic, it has also been hard to bring some of these memories back to the forefront of my mind. I had buried the memory of some of these sad events that I had gone through. After writing about it, though, I feel lighter, better than I did before. It has been worth it. Writing has also helped me to see things in a better perspective, a much more mature perspective than I had at the time when some of these events took place. I have been able to reflect on these events and gain more clarity and acceptance. This process has helped me to dig deep into things that I had buried in my heart, but it has been good to resurrect those memories and understand a bit better how I felt at the time. I believe by doing this, I have been able to release those memories and feelings and be better for it.

I would hope that others who read my books would be encouraged to move forward, not without their loved ones but with the capacity to keep them in their hearts, as they will always be part of us. I have learnt that it is important to have some coping mechanisms in place to help you get through each day, week, month, and year.

I regularly meet with friends for coffee, lunch, or dinner. It is one of the things that keeps me going. I have also become very active in my church since I took voluntary redundancy from my previous employer of eighteen years. I am part of the church's Bereavement Support team, as I want to be able to help others, just as another local bereavement group helped me when I first lost Marley. I can share with others what was beneficial for me and what was not. Hopefully some of this information can be useful to others. I share a lot about my grieving process in my second book, *Living Without Marley*.

Just as I have had the opportunity to listen to others in similar situations, I have also read books by others sharing the story of how they pulled through their loss. I have also prayed with some and just spent time with others as they navigate their grief. Helping others by simply walking beside them as they navigate their grief journey can be very helpful. It counteracts that innate helplessness that all of us feel when we lose someone. You feel like there is something you could have done to prevent them from passing, which of course, in most or all cases, there isn't.

I try to plan different things to look forward to. That is one of the many coping mechanisms that I took from my first bereavement support group. I plan regular spa days or outings to the theatre to see a play or hear a musical concert. Sometimes it's something as effortless as joining the ladies in church for Saturday morning walks. When I can, I also travel, visiting family and friends in different countries. Last year I went to Stockholm in Sweden with two of my close friends. I had been to Stockholm a lot previously though each time it was for business, never for leisure. It was good to go as a tourist and to take time to see all the landmarks. This year I also visited Krakow in Poland, another country that I had been to a lot for business but never for pleasure.

It was great to be able to take in all the rich history of Krakow with my own very personal guide, my friend Joanna.

I don't know what the future holds, but I definitely will embrace it as I have done in the past and the present. I would like to continue helping children and young people with mental health conditions, and I would like to continue giving support to parents and caregivers who are going through grief and loss similar to mine. I would also like to continue to share my experiences with others if it would give them strength, comfort, and hope.

I am a Christian believer, and I could not write this book without sharing about the goodness of God. Despite everything that I have experienced, I believe in God. Even with all the other coping mechanisms that I have, without God I would not be strong. If you are of a different faith, I applaud you and encourage you to open your heart and let God speak to you. If you have no faith at all, try to keep an open heart for God to speak to you.

Lastly, I would like to let you know that no matter what you may have gone through or are currently going through, He cares. God cares for you. He cares about the little things that upset you the same way He cares about the big things that upset you. He promises to never abandon us. As it says in Deuteronomy 31:8:

"It is the Lord who goes before you; He will be with you. He will not fail you or abandon you. Do not fear or be dismayed."

Trust Him because He cares.

15

Epilogue: Three Years & Nine Months Later

Today is my fourth birthday without Marley. As I said in the last chapter, I always plan to spend my birthday in a meaningful way as I celebrate the day I was born and will continue to do so every year. Most birthdays have been small but meaningful celebrations whilst for significant milestones, there have been bigger celebrations.

Today my plan was to spend the day with one of my close friends in London, having a makeover and a photo shoot. The itinerary had been planned, the train tickets bought, and the pickup time agreed upon. We drove to the train station with plenty of time to get a parking ticket and make our way to the platform. But I happened to look towards the barriers and saw a small group of people talking to the station attendants. I pointed this out to my friend as she was busy purchasing the parking ticket with her phone. She asked me to go ahead and see what was going on.

I was not expecting to suddenly be thrown back to the traumatic loss of Marley. The station attendant had closed the barriers so no one could get through with their train tickets because someone had jumped onto the track and been hit by a fast-moving train. This had happened about a few miles before our station. All trains were cancelled for the foreseeable future. I looked across to the other side of the station and saw a group of police officers and paramedics. It was like flashback to December 2020 when I had had to call the paramedics for Marley.

I was really distraught. My empathy kicked in as I started thinking of this person and the family and friends who would be receiving the sad and traumatic news that their loved one had ended their life. I became quite emotional because it was the last thing I expected to happen on my birthday. With the train cancelled, we had to find another way of getting to London.

We succeeded in getting an Uber for a very reasonable price, and whilst we were in the Uber on our way to London, I called the studio to let them know that we might not make our appointment. They were very understanding and advised us to let them know if we would be delayed for more than five minutes once we got to London, so that they could reschedule us for an hour later at no additional charge. In the midst of this sad situation I asked God, *Why did this happen? Why did this person feel so low that they thought they could not last another week, even another day, and had to end their life?* God cares was what was being impressed in my heart.

I want to appeal to anyone who has suicidal thoughts or experiences low moods or feelings of worthlessness: ending your life is not the answer. In some ways it transfers a burden to your loved ones. The impact of your action will stay with your family and friends forever. It is irreversible and there is no do over. Your family and friends will have to live with this burden for the rest of their lives. And as it happened with me, they might relive the whole traumatic experience again and again if they know of someone else who has lost their life by suicide. The answer to suicidal thoughts, low moods, and feelings of worthlessness is to get help. Speak to your family or to a close friend and let them support you through your difficult times.

I thank God that, because He cares and is a loving God, I went on to enjoy the rest of my birthday. But there was certainly that part of me that continued to grieve for another life lost by suicide.

Please reach out to any organisations that can help and support you if you do not want to speak to your friends or family.

About the Author

Majendi Jarrett is a Christian author and speaker. She is the author of *Marley's Memoir: The Journey to an Irreversible Action and the Aftermath* and *Living Without Marley*. She often speaks at churches, schools, and corporate events. She is a graduate of Fourah Bay College in Freetown, Sierra Leone, and the University of Bedfordshire in the United Kingdom. She started writing in 2019 and published her first book in 2022, with a focus on real-life experiences. She currently lives in Bedfordshire with her husband, son, and a pond of tropical fish.